PASSION AND PA

Passion and Paranoia
Emotions and the Culture of Emotion in Academia

CHARLOTTE BLOCH
University of Copenhagen, Denmark

LONDON AND NEW YORK

First published 2012 by Ashgate Publishing

2 Park Square, Milton Park, Abingdon, Oxon OX14 4RN
711 Third Avenue, New York, NY 10017, USA

Routledge is an imprint of the Taylor & Francis Group, an informa business

First issued in paperback 2016

Copyright © 2012 Charlotte Bloch

Charlotte Bloch has asserted her right under the Copyright, Designs and Patents Act, 1988, to be identified as the author of this work.

Originally published in Danish as *Passion og Paranoia: Følelser og følelseskultur i Akademia*, Syddansk Universitetsforlag, 2007.

All rights reserved. No part of this book may be reprinted or reproduced or utilised in any form or by any electronic, mechanical, or other means, now known or hereafter invented, including photocopying and recording, or in any information storage or retrieval system, without permission in writing from the publishers.

Notice:
Product or corporate names may be trademarks or registered trademarks, and are used only for identification and explanation without intent to infringe.

British Library Cataloguing in Publication Data
Bloch, Charlotte.
  Passion and paranoia : emotions and the culture of emotion
in academia.
  1. Scholars--Professional relationships. 2. College
teachers--Professional relationships. 3. Learning and
scholarship--Social aspects. 4. Learning and scholarship--
Psychological aspects.
  I. Title
  378.1'2-dc23

Library of Congress Cataloging-in-Publication Data
Bloch, Charlotte.
  Passion and paranoia : emotions and the culture of emotion in academia / by Charlotte Bloch.
    p. cm.
  Includes bibliographical references and index.
  ISBN 978-1-4094-4254-7 (hardback)
1. Emotions--Sociological aspects. I. Title.
  HM1033.B58 2012
  152.4--dc23
                                                            2012014352

ISBN 978-1-4094-4254-7 (hbk)
ISBN 978-1-138-25035-2 (pbk)

Contents

Preface *vii*

1	Introduction	1
2	Theory and Empirical Basis	7
3	A Huge Emotional Challenge	17
4	The Order of Visibility	37
5	The Janus Face of the Peer Review	55
6	The Politics of Laughter	71
7	The Academic Lunchroom	85
8	Social Bonds in Academia	97
9	Emotional Micropolitics and Gender	113
10	Conclusion and Perspectives	135

References *143*
Index *151*

Preface

This book is about the socio-emotional world of Academia. The English text is a translated and revised version of the original Danish edition published in 2007. The main content of the Danish and English editions is more or less identical. Although the basic argument of the book remains unchanged, the English edition contains some additions and elaborations. Chapter 1 has been extended with some reflections on international trends in university systems, while Chapter 10 has been expanded to include a theoretical discussion of the potential effects of the modernisation of university life on the quality of research. Furthermore, a new chapter on socio-emotional processes in the academic lunchroom has been added. This is a revised version of a chapter published earlier in a Swedish anthology entitled 'Det sociale livets emotionella grunder' (*The Emotional Foundations of Social Life*). When possible, references to Scandinavian literature have been supplemented by references to English language literature. Quotations from text that has not been written in or previously translated to English have been translated by the translators and myself.

The results of this work have been presented in a number of contexts: Nordic and European universities, The Research Network for Sociology of Emotions, under the European Sociological Association (ESA), and other research conferences. I am indebted to my colleagues as well as a number of fellow academics for their helpful and inspiring comments. I am also indebted to Anne Lise Dalsgård and Catherine Hasse for their assistance in the interview phase of this work.

I am grateful to the Danish Research Councils, who provided financial support to the research project behind this book.

Special thanks are due to the Department of Sociology, University of Copenhagen, which has provided financial support for the translation of this book to English.

Last, but not least, I am indebted to Katherine O'Doherty Jensen for her valuable contribution. She not only read the proofs of the English translation with a sharp eye for both form and content, but also helped to clarify certain aspects and ensured the nuanced stringency of the final text.

Finally, I am grateful to my husband Jan Ulrik Secher who never fails to encourage me in every aspect of my work, including this project.

Chapter 1

Introduction

> We can see it on someone just passing by – those flushed cheeks – when things are going really well. Now things are happening and with real passion. There's not much difference between the feeling you have when you're in love and the feeling you have when your research is going really well. It's a little bit sacred – just like when you're in love. (woman, assistant professor)

> He was angry, disappointed and upset by the assessment committee's recommendation, but he was also extremely incensed and quite beside himself...In the end, he declared that he would not speak one more word to me ever again. Since then – and that was [some] years ago – he has looked right through me whenever we met, and we have never said hello to each other. (man, associate professor)

These excerpts are taken from my study of emotions in Academia.[1] The first describes the special passion and excitement that can be involved in doing research. The second describes the strong feelings of anger, disappointment and irreconcilable hatred that can arise when colleagues evaluate, criticise and assess each other's work.

According to their statutes, universities must produce and disseminate knowledge at the highest scientific level. For this purpose, the university has a particular organisational structure, a particular culture and a particular career path. The structure, culture and career ladder can be seen as the tools of the organisation, which serve to ensure not only outstanding research, but also the selection of the best candidates. This process of selection can be seen as funnel-shaped. At the top, PhD students come pouring in, but the funnel narrows quickly, since competition is tough at every stage of the process; it never stops, many are rejected and only a few get through to a further academic career.

The university as an organisation must generate excellent research. However, since the organisational structures at issue are peopled by mere human beings, these structures also activate a range of emotions that affect collegial relationships, research activities, the research environment and the self-esteem of individuals. As indicated by the excerpts above, research as an activity can be intoxicating, giving rise to a sense of delight and involvement, but competition also nurtures envy, mistrust and malice, just as colleagues' assessments of each other's work can give rise to anger, disappointment, bitterness and broken bonds. These emotions are not so much evoked by the personalities of individuals as by the character of particular social structures and social relations, as the coming chapters will show.

---

1 The term Academia is used to describe research-based institutions of higher education, i.e. universities, university centres and university colleges.

The university world is generally associated with rationality, methodological principles, objectivity and logical argument. From the point of view of this organisational self-understanding, emotions appear to be alien, irrelevant and disruptive. However, this does not mean that Academia does not have a culture of emotions. The perception of emotions as being alien and irrelevant is in fact the expression of a particular culture of emotions. In this case, an academic culture in which no feelings have place.

Within the area of organisational research, there has been increasing focus in recent decades on the importance of emotions in organisations (Fineman 1993, 2000, Albrow 1997, Flam 2002, Nyend and Wennes 2005). Organisations are rational structures, but also emotional structures. In the words of Albrow (1992: 326), affectivity is a key dimension of organisational performance. This awareness has not penetrated to Academia, just as emotions and the cultural norms that regulate them are not described in either older or more recent sociology of science (Barnes 1972, Bourdieu 1988, Nowotny and Taschwer 1996 and Becher and Trowler 2001).

The excerpts above illustrate the range and intensity of emotions, and university life embraces many such strong emotions. Emotions move us, but we also seek to adapt them to prevailing cultural norms. We may not talk about our feelings, try not to show them at all, but they are there, and they do have effects. Some groups are better than others at handling their emotions within the boundaries of a culture of silence; some can make strategic use of emotions in furthering their careers, while others hide their emotions by means of withdrawal. Thus, emotions and the ways in which we handle them constitute key dimensions of academic life and, for better or worse, they contribute to the character of its social relationships, and to inclusion in or exclusion from an academic career path.[2]

In order to throw light upon what emotions mean for academic life, and what these emotions reveal about Academia as an organisation, I have interviewed PhD fellows, assistant professors, associate professors and full professors, focussing on the particular social emotions of anger, pride, joy, shame and laughter. These academic groups articulate different aspects of the emotional life of Academia. However, I also dig beyond the narratives of these interviewees. Emotions arise within contexts, and therefore sociological theories of emotions are used to demonstrate the interplay between social structures and emotions, and between emotions and a culture of emotions. These theories are important because they help to bring us beyond the prevalent tendency in western cultures to understand emotions as intra-personal phenomena within the individual as such. Chapter 2 presents the theoretical framework that structures my analysis. This framework is based on two dimensions of analysis: a structural dimension, referring to the social organisation of Academia, and a cultural dimension, referring to the norms,

---

[2] In general, the term 'feelings' connotes fewer or milder physical sensations than does the term 'emotions'. Feeling in this sense is a milder form of emotion. For the purpose of this book these two terms are used interchangeably. (cf. Hochschild 1983: 244)

values and discourses of academic life. The narratives of these academic groups are interpreted and analysed on the basis of this theoretical framework. In addition, specific theories are employed at certain points in order to penetrate further into the perspectives of these narratives. It must be said that Chapter 2 is a highly theoretical chapter, and can be omitted by more empirically inclined readers.

The academic groups under consideration here hold different positions in the academic hierarchy, just as they articulate different aspects of emotional life in Academia. Chapter 3 gives voice to PhD fellows. They are the newcomers and they must learn how to relate to the emotions of Academia. They describe the emotions of research as activity, but also the feelings related to their position at the bottom of the hierarchical power structure. PhD fellows describe socialisation to Academia as constituting 'a huge emotional challenge'. The chapter also describes the different types of emotion work undertaken by PhD fellows.

In Chapter 4 we take a step further into Academia, listening to the voices of assistant professors. The plot of this chapter concerns the interplay between emotions, academic norms regarding emotions, and the struggle for the 'right' kind of visibility in the fight for recognition and for one's career. The games played in this endeavour are captured by such concepts as 'the politics of friendliness', 'the deceiving game' and 'ventriloquism'. The deceiving game refers to the facade behind which the fear of critical assessment of one's research on the part of colleagues is kept hidden, while 'ventriloquism' describes the special ways in which the yearning for recognition and the prohibition against displaying pride in Academia, are tackled.

In Chapter 5, we approach the emotions related to what Pierre Bourdieu considers the central nerve of academic practice, the 'peer review'. In this chapter, we hear the voices of associate professors and professors for the most part. Based on their accounts, the concept of 'assessor anger' is introduced. In addition, the negative emotions that arise when peer reviews are perceived as being offensive are described, as well as the emotions generated by the university's meritocratic structure: mistrust, envy and *schadenfreude*. These are familiar, but prohibited, emotions within the academic culture of emotions, and for this reason attempts are made to keep them hidden from the eyes of colleagues.

Academia is a setting for all kinds of emotions, including joy, fun, humour and laughter. Chapter 6 shows how irritation with unreasonable supervisors, the frustrations of research and the burden of competitive relationships are redeemed by laughter and humour. On these points, we hear stories from the bottom and the top of the academic hierarchy. At the PhD level, a 'ground floor' humour is described – collective poking fun at authorities and objects of authority. At the assistant and associate professor levels, 'joking relationships' are described as playful, teasing or competitive ways of relating to others.

Social processes that connect or divide are found in Academia, and both of these processes are encountered in the academic lunchroom. Based on Simmel's theory of the meal as a social form, it is shown how the lunch setting generates fellowship and solidarity. However, the manner in which formal and informal hierarchies penetrate conversation in the lunchroom is also shown, exemplified by a professor's right to decide upon the topic of conversation. Chapter 7 illustrates ways in which different academic groups contribute to connecting and dividing processes in the lunchroom. This chapter also illustrates ways in which these processes can become entangled by humour, ventriloquism and forms of gift-exchange.

The following two chapters constitute meta-analyses of the kinds of feelings and relationships that have been presented in the preceding chapters. Here the work of the American sociologist, Thomas Scheff, regarding the theory of non-conscious emotional dynamics and social bonds is employed. Chapter 8 pursues these emotional dynamics, and their significance for the character of social relationships and communication among researchers are discussed. It is argued that the structures of Academia give rise to damaged social bonds, which have lasting consequences for the character and quality of communication. Assistant, associate and full professors' own assessments of social relationships in Academia are also described.

Chapter 9 introduces the theory of the American sociologist, Candace Clark, regarding emotional micropolitics. Clark focuses on the relationship between self-feelings and social standing, and on the ways in which we practise emotional micropolitics in our handling of our own emotions and those of others. A distinction is drawn between politics directed at gaining a better position in the microhierarchy, and politics directed at creating equal social standing within cooperative relationships. It is argued that the academic culture of emotions legitimises emotional micropolitics that generate hierarchical relations. This theory is employed to highlight the different ways in which men and women handle the emotions of academic life, and it is shown how gendered emotional norms give men access to these hierarchical emotional micropolitics, while women are referred to micropolitics that contribute to their relative invisibility in social and academic terms.

In the final chapter, I briefly summarise the results of this study and discuss its further implications. What do emotions tell us about academic life? The structures of Academia give rise to particular emotions, but how do these affect the quality of research? How do dominant political trends regarding education and research affect emotional life in Academia and the emotions of research?

It should be noted that this book about the socio-emotional world of academic life is based upon data drawn from universities and other research-based institutions of higher education in Denmark. University systems in the Western world differ in regard to their national and historical roots. But they also share a number of common characteristics arising from their shared cultural history, including the legacy of the Enlightenment, and which are expressed in concepts regarding the autonomy of the university as an institution, the freedom of research and the peer review as the measure of the quality of published research. These values cut across national boundaries and differences. Accordingly, these are the values that have been defended when new educational policies and new initiatives regarding research policy have been on the agenda in different parts of the Western world in recent decades. This book takes its point of departure in the structures and cultural conceptions of modern research-based universities, which are internationally recognised and which transcend national boundaries. Its focus, however, is not upon systems and structures as such, but rather upon the socio-emotional processes to which they give rise, and which in turn these processes serve to sustain.

Chapter 2
Theory and Empirical Basis

This chapter presents the scientific basis for my analysis. I speak about emotions, but what exactly are emotions, and how are they embedded in the organisation and culture of Academia? How have I studied this field, and what is the empirical basis for my discussion of emotions? I present some theoretical approaches to emotions first, followed by my analytical model and the empirical basis for my study. I close the chapter with a general description of the research environments.

Theoretical Framework

Three approaches to research regarding emotions can be distinguished: biological, interactional and discursive-constructivist approaches. The biological approach understands emotions as being universal biological impulses, each of which is released by particular stimuli, and has a specific type of expression as well as a behavioural dimension.[1] The discursive-constructivist approach understands emotions as being discursive cultural constructions. They may have a biological basis, but are first and foremost seen as being founded on cultural and moral interpretations.[2] Between these two extremes lies the interactional approach, which recognises a biological basis for emotions, but focuses primarily on the formative influence of culture upon emotions, which is exerted by means of norms.[3]

Sociological theories of emotions draw on biological and interactional approaches. Some theories concern the relation between social/structural conditions and emotions. These theories understand emotions as dispositions to act and draw on the biological approach. Other theories focus on the cultural regulation of emotions by means of feeling rules and the emotion work undertaken

---

1 This tradition has its roots in the theory of William James (1884), according to which feelings are our perceptions of biological changes that are released by certain stimuli.

2 The discursive-constructivist approach to emotions has been developed primarily within anthropology and psychology. Catherine Lutz (1988), Lila Abu-Lughod (1991) and Rom Harré (1986) are important representatives of this approach. See also Bloch (2001: 40) for a more detailed presentation of this tradition.

3 The concept 'interactional' refers to the assumption that biological and socio-cultural factors are closely interwoven in the formation of emotions. The concept is thus not synonymous with symbolic interactionism, but can embrace elements of the latter tradition. This definition is based on Williams (1998: 135, note 2).

by individuals. They take their point of departure in the interactional approach to emotions and emphasise the significance of emotions as information to the self.

Organisations have both structures and cultures, and I therefore draw on both structural and cultural theories of emotions in order to elucidate the interplay between emotions, structures and culture in Academia. My approach to emotions in Academia is accordingly based on two dimensions of analysis: a structural dimension focussing on the interplay between structures, social relations and emotions; and a cultural dimension focussing on the interplay between emotions, emotional culture and individuals' handling of emotions.

The Structural Dimension

Organisations have social structures, which serve as the basis of power and status distinctions in social relations. Sociological theories of emotions have examined the relationship between power and status relations on the one hand and emotions on the other, but they have not specifically concerned the social structures of Academia. For this reason, I have drawn on the French sociologist Pierre Bourdieu's analyses of Academia and the scientific field. Although Bourdieu has not examined emotions, he does give us insight into the social structure of Academia. When combined with sociological theory of emotions, his analysis can shed light on specific relationships between the social structure of Academia and the emotions characteristic of academic life.

Bourdieu (1975) emphasises two structures as being characteristic of Academia: a specific structure and a hierarchical power structure with meritocratic traits. The *specific structure* is unique to Academia, compared with other social fields. It is characteristic of this structure that the clients of its producers (researchers) are primarily competing colleagues, that is to say, other researchers. Scientific recognition, which is the basis of merit in Academia, is accorded by other researchers who, in principle, are also competitors. This structure is manifested in the 'peer review', whereby specialists in a given field of research assess the value of each other's work. This particular structure ensures a critical review of the work produced by colleagues (competitors). The peer review is the backbone of Academia. In principle, it is the key to achieving merit, which in turn gives access to Academia's other structure: the *hierarchical power structure*. This structure is analysed as a social field of positions, defined by different volumes of academic and scientific capital.[4] Within this field, there is unrelenting competition for merit, which increases one's capital and thereby one's power to influence academic

---

4 Academic capital or power is materialised by holding important posts in the managerial hierarchy, education policy committees, commissions, etc., while scientific capital is materialised in research management, membership of scientific bodies and research councils, in publications, translations of one's work to other languages, citations in citation indexes, etc. These types of capital create the basis for power hierarchies of different types (Bourdieu 1988).

practice. This competition unfolds within a series of ranked dimensions: number of publications, number of citations in different citation indexes, relative prestige of periodicals and publishers, size of project grants, number of PhD fellows to be supervised, etc. At the top of the hierarchy, rivalry concerns which research paradigms constitute science, the size of project grants and the number of PhD fellows. At the bottom of the hierarchy there is rivalry for attention, any project funds at all, the relevance of projects to core research areas of the department, etc. In principle, this struggle for position, or rivalry, is founded on meritocratic principles in the sense that position is based on merit (rather than social background, gender, etc.), and is recognised as the expression of shared and sustained values.

Academia legitimises its inclusion and exclusion practices by applying meritocratic principles. According to Bourdieu, however, these practices are also based on other criteria. Moreover, the paradigms within which research is undertaken and assessed also constitute a central battleground in Academia.[5]

Summing up, Bourdieu's analysis pinpoints two social structures in Academia: the specific structure whereby colleagues at one and the same time are each other's judges and competitors, and the hierarchical power structure that is legitimised by means of meritocratic principles and assumptions.

These social structures are theoretically anchored constructions that serve to highlight structural dynamics. The structural relations at issue can neither be reduced to nor directly inferred from the concrete social interactions of participants. This is not to say, however, that these social structures are without significance for interaction between participants. On the contrary, they are of significance and, according to Bourdieu (1975: 19), they constitute the framework within which social relations and concrete interactions occur.

The American sociologists Randahl Collins (1990, 2004) and Theodor Kemper (1978a, 1978b, 1982, 2002) have developed theories regarding the interplay between power and status relations as experienced and different emotions. Emotions are provoked by "Real, anticipated, imagined, or recollected outcomes of social relationships" (Kemper 1978a: 32), emotions are dispositions to act, and emotions provide the link between structure and actor (Barbalet 2002: 4).[6]

---

5 In Academia, the fundamental struggle is to attain monopoly of the definition of what science is (Bourdieu 1975: 19).

6 Both Kemper and Collins, who are the main theoreticians within the structural tradition, examine theoretical prototypes at the level of concrete interactions, and see these interactions as building blocks of social structure. They therefore equate aggregated micro-interactions and structures (Kemper and Collins 1990). There is thus an apparent theoretical contradiction between the micro-interaction approach, represented by structural sociologies of the emotions, and Bourdieu's structural approach to interaction. In the analysis undertaken here, these two approaches are treated as mutually complementary. The micro-interaction approach has certain limitations, but its strength lies in its focus upon the interplay of emotions, power and status relations in social interactions. Bourdieu's strength lies in his structural perspective, but there are also limitations with regard to an analysis of the interplay between field and dispositions to act.

Candace Clark has developed the theory of how we create social microhierarchies by means of emotional micropolitics, and Thomas Scheff has developed theory regarding the relationship between deference, disrespect, emotions and social bonds. These theories are presented in later chapters and are used to unravel the dynamic relationships between the two structures of Academia and emotions.

The Cultural Dimension

Historically, organisations can be viewed as ways of orienting and stabilising passions, feelings and sensibilities, which have otherwise existed in a non-organised form (Flam 1990a, 1990b, 2002).[7] Passions are stabilised by rational organisations. When such organisations have been established, they construct norms regarding feelings by means of rules and procedures. These constructed emotions differ from, but are related to, the original emotions that set the whole process in motion. On this point, Flam introduces the concept of *representative emotions*, which are the emotions that present the organisation's particular goals, values and self-image.

Modern Academia is an organisation that is historically rooted in the tension between the Enlightenment's thirst for knowledge and the constricting dogmas of the religious world view of that time. This entails that Academia is historically constituted by distinguishing the spheres of science and religion, by distinguishing systematic method, specialisation and objectivity on the one hand and traditional religious awareness based on passion, faith and feelings on the other.[8] These historical roots can be interpreted as providing the basis for a culture of emotions, the representative emotions of which are actually an 'absence of feelings'. The concept of representative emotions refers to emotions that present the organisation's goals, values and self-image. The American sociologist Arlie Hochschild has developed a theory of how our emotions are formed by cultural conceptions and values. She draws a distinction regarding cultural norms between feeling rules and expression rules. *Feeling rules* refer to emotions that the culture prescribes as appropriate to a given context, while *expression rules* refer to norms regarding how, and the extent to which, the emotions in question should be expressed. We may feel as the situation prescribes, but there can also be a discrepancy between what we feel and what we ought to feel. It can therefore be necessary to undertake *emotion work,* which involves the processing of our emotions in order to adapt them to prevailing feeling rules.[9]

---

7 Flam builds on the work of Max Weber (1930/1995).

8 Science is historically based on concepts of objectivity, measurability, etc. The philosopher of science, Lorraine Daston (1995), argues that, historically, these ideas and requirements are based on so-called emotion-saturated values (moral economy). Quantification as a procedure, for example, expresses the prising of unlimited communication between scientists.

9 Hochschild distinguishes between emotion work and emotional labour. The latter refers to the processing of one's own emotions in a paid/waged context of work with a

The existing literature includes little reference to emotions and their normative regulation in research organisations. In my analysis of the accounts of these matters offered by PhD fellows, assistant professors and associate professors, the concepts developed by Flam and Hochschild are used as analytical tools to illuminate feeling rules and norms regarding the handling and expression of emotions.

Feeling Processes

As stated, structural and cultural theories understand emotions in different ways. Structural theories have a biologically based understanding of emotions, while cultural theories focus on the adaptation of our emotions to cultural norms.[10] I use both structural and cultural theories as analytical tools regarding emotions in Academia. Yet I do not subscribe to the view that emotions are biologically based essential features of individuals, nor do I believe that emotions can be reduced to linguistically discursive constructions. Emotions arise within contexts, and thereby within a social and cultural reality in which we already take part. Emotions mediate between us and a given social reality. They involve affect, cognition, assessment, motivation and the body. Many of our emotions are immediate, pre-reflective or semi-conscious signals and dispositions to act.[11] Furthermore, emotions are relatively autonomous. There are limits to their plasticity, and emotions have their own dynamics, which enter our lives in silent, unnoticed ways.[12] Tensions can therefore arise between emotions and a given culture of emotions. This field of tension can be handled in different ways. Emotions can be expressed as they are felt or they can be moderated by the culture, depending on a) the strength of existing expression rules; b) the strength and type of the felt emotion, c) individual differences in the capacity and motivation to feel and to express the emotion, and d) the structure of the given situation (Gibson 1997: 234).

Figure 2.1 is a graphic presentation of the conceptual framework employed in my analysis. This framework includes a structural dimension focusing on social

---

view to generating particular emotions in others. See Hochschild (1983) for a more detailed account of these concepts.

10 Reservations should be made regarding a sharp distinction between biological and cultural approaches to emotions. Hochschild, whom I regard as a representative of the cultural approach, recognises a biological basis and sees emotions as signals in the sense of coded impulses to act. The cultural-interactional approach does not thus exclude emotions as dispositions to act, but focuses specifically on emotions as informative signals for assessment regarding for example danger, joy or jealousy.

11 According to Barbalet (2004), tacit, unattended emotions constitute the largest group of emotions. Barbalet refers to the research of Antonio Damasio (2000), which shows how unconscious emotions affect our social life.

12 Scheff's analysis (1994) of spirals of emotion and the effects on social relations of unacknowledged shame provides an example of the intrinsic dynamics of emotions. Reference should also be made to Craib's discussion (1998) of particular emotional dynamics that are overlooked in constructivist approaches to emotions.

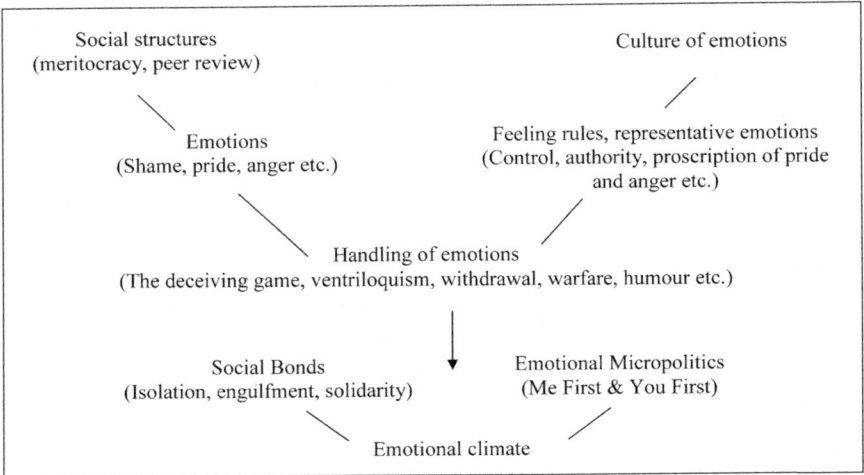

Figure 2.1   Conceptual framework

structures, social relations and emotions, and a cultural dimension focusing on culture of emotions and feeling rules. My analysis examines the friction between emotions and feeling rules, bringing the two analytical dimensions together in the concept of handling emotions. The handling of emotions is interpreted not only in terms of individuals' adaptation of their emotions to feeling rules, but also as actions by means of which bonding and microhierarchies are created. The concepts shown in Figure 2.1 are merely analytical categories. In life as lived, emotions, feeling rules, emotion management, social bonds and emotional micropolitics are interwoven in complex ways. I have not had the opportunity to study these processes as living processes, having relied upon accounts given by interviewees. This means that I have interpreted the linguistically mediated expressions of these processes. This is a limitation of the interview method, but such are the conditions of analysis. We cannot reach the lived emotions of others and their processes in an unmediated form.

Material and Methods[13]

As already indicated, my study of emotions in Academia is based on interviews with PhD fellows, assistant professors, associate professors and full professors. There

---

13   The present study constituted part of a research initiative funded by the Research Councils of Denmark, entitled 'Gender Barriers in Higher Education and Research' and conducted during the period 1996–2002. This study was a sub-project within the project entitled 'Gender in Academic Organization' undertaken by Charlotte Bloch, Cathrine Hasse, Inge Henningsen, Lis Højgård, Hanne Nexø Jensen and Dorte Marie Søndergård.

are many different emotions in Academia. I focus particularly on the organisation of research, and I therefore opted to focus my interviews upon four groups of basic relational emotions, as follows: a) pride/joy, b) anger, c) shame/embarrassment/confusion, and 4) laughter.[14] What can these emotions tell us about life in Academia?

To illuminate these issues, I interviewed 54 people selected on the basis of gender and academic position from the faculties of health sciences, social sciences and humanities.[15] Each faculty was represented by an equal number of women and men, distributed by position held, i.e., PhD fellows, assistant professors and associate professors/full professors. Since many university staff members are known to the public, the requirement to ensure anonymity was accordingly strong. For this reason, interviewees were recruited from different departments and institutions of higher education throughout Denmark. Data collection comprised personal face-to-face interviews with the assistant professor and associate professor/full professor groups. Focus group interviews were undertaken with PhD fellows in faculty-based focus groups, men and women comprising separate groups in each case. All interviews were phenomenologically oriented, being designed to elicit descriptions of concrete examples of the four emotion groups. Interviewees were asked about the processing and management of their emotions, with a view to elucidating the relationship between emotions and the prevailing culture of emotions. They were also asked about emotional micropolitics, that is, ways to improve their position in everyday microhierarchies by displaying specific emotions or by provoking these in others. Finally, interviewees were asked to assess their relationships with colleagues in terms of the extent to which these were respectively 'nourishing' or 'wearing'.[16]

All interview material was transcribed, and interpretation and analysis based on the interplay between sociological theories of the emotions and the empirical material.[17]

The programme was jointly financed by the Research Councils for Social Sciences, Humanities, Natural Sciences and Health Sciences (each of which now constitutes part of the Danish Council for Independent Research).

14   Relational emotions are emotions that arise within social relations. These emotions can have the self as object, for example pride, shame or guilt, or they can have the other person as object, for example anger, respect or admiration. A given emotion, such as anger or fear, can be, but is not necessarily, a relational emotion. For example, the fear one can feel when peering down into a dark lift shaft, or the anger and irritation felt on bumping into a chair, are not relational emotions. See Shott (1979) and Clark (1990) for a discussion of relational emotions.

15   The interviewees were selected by consulting departmental websites. They were then contacted by telephone and invited to participate in the study. The rate of non-response was minimal.

16   In the Danish language, these concepts constitute a rhyming pair ('nærende' or 'tærende') and are a familiar feature of everyday discourse.

17   The interview material was analysed by means of phenomenological-hermeneutic interpretation. This entails explicitation of meanings based on the interplay between the

Urban and Rural Research Environments

Within the sociology of science, distinctions are made between different types of research cultures (Snow 1959, Knorr Cetina 1999, Becker and Trowler 2001). With regard to research cultures, this study comprised staff from three different faculties: social sciences, humanities and health sciences. However, the scope of the empirical material is too limited to admit differentiation between the research cultures of different faculties. I present a different distinction made by Becker and Trowler (2001), which cuts across these faculties and concerns so-called 'urban' and 'rural' research environments. This distinction does not concern urban and rural settings, but rather population density within different areas of research. In so-called urban environments, population density is high insofar as research is focussed within a limited area characterised by few salient and clearly defined problems for investigation. In rural environments, population density is low in the sense that researchers typically cover a broader area of intellectual territory embracing many different themes.

Rural and urban research environments create conditions for different types of competitive relationships between colleagues. An urban environment is characterised by frequently intense competition to be the first to publish results. This relationship generates emotions such as fear and suspicion among colleagues. People keep their cards close to their chests, sometimes publish results too quickly and tend to worry about theft of intellectual property. This type of competition does not arise in rural environments, in which researchers are engaged in working on a wide range of different and unrelated topics. But this does not entail that competition does not arise in rural environments. It is simply not expressed in the form of rapid publication of results, but rather in more subtle ways such as seeking to promote one's own publications, behaving aggressively at meetings and maintaining a high degree of single-mindedness. People seek to outdo each other in terms of the quality and significance of their work, while seldom competing within the same area.

The settings in which this study was undertaken can be characterised as primarily rural research environments. Although a few interviewees from the health sciences represented urban research environments, the majority of interviewees from this field in fact belonged to research groups that I have interpreted as being rural research environments. As already indicated Becher and Trowler's distinction between 'rural' and 'urban' is not a distinction between faculties as such. For example, a research centre within the humanities might be devoted to the work

---

analysis of units of meaning in a given narrative and their interpretation in the light of the narrative as a whole. Interpretation also included non-verbal and verbal signals that, according to Scheff, can be markers of emotions. For an overview of verbal and non-verbal emotional markers, see Retzinger (1991), Bloch (1996) and Gottschalk et al. (1969). For a more detailed account of the phenomenological-hermeneutic interpretation method, see Giorgi (1975, 1992) and Bloch (2001).

of a particular author such as Søren Kierkegaard or Hans Christian Andersen, in which researchers are engaged in a limited field of investigation, and in which the research environment is more urban than rural. This study primarily concerns rural research environments.

Chapter 3
A Huge Emotional Challenge

PhD fellows form the base of the academic organisation, and this base is expanding. They are to be trained, but also socialised and assessed in terms of a potential research career.[1]

Several studies of the ways in which PhD fellows assimilate academic culture have been undertaken (Gerholm and Gerholm 1992, Abbel 2000, 2003, Ehn and Löfgren 2004). These studies do not concern emotions and the emotional culture of Academia.

PhD fellows are located at the bottom of the academic hierarchy, i.e. in a position from which the hierarchical power structure is experienced from the bottom up. In addition, they are newcomers and have the outsider's ability to discern the tacit emotional demands of academic life.

I have identified three emotional axes around which PhD fellows' self-esteem and belief in their projects revolve. The first axis, which I call the 'emotions of research', concerns research as an activity. The two other axes, 'emotions of the supervisor relationship' and 'emotions of the power structure', are related to the research organisation.

Emotions of Research

Research is an activity that involves the whole person. This applies to all researchers, but is perhaps especially pronounced at the PhD level. This is because PhD life is particularly focussed upon research, and because PhD fellows have limited experience of the character of research. Research entails passion, but is also a special activity that concerns the 'not yet known'. Research is based on belief, trust and hope, but also on the experience of resistant challenges and related

---

1 A Danish PhD fellowship is a three-year appointment that includes courses of study, a stay abroad, limited teaching obligations and the completion of a thesis. The PhD degree constitutes the formal admission ticket to a career in research at universities and other institutions of higher education, but is also the basis for employment in other parts of the public sector as well as the private sector. PhD programmes vary from country to country, as well as between departments, and have changed over time. None the less, the programme includes the same elements: a recruitment basis, a span of time, coursework, teaching obligations and the completion of a thesis.

feelings of uncertainty and doubt.[2] Am I on the right track or is this a dead end? PhD fellows identify with their projects. As one of them says:

> For me, my project is quite simply a way of life. It is my life, and I identify with it completely (laughs).[3]

Accordingly, the successes and failures of project work can give rise to severe fluctuations in self-esteem.

> When the experiments don't work it really eats you up inside. And the longer things don't work out, the more it eats you up, and in the end, if nothing has worked for half a year, then... I spent several years working on certain experiments. Nothing worked out at all, and I was on the point of going to the dogs – really! You just get so desperate and frustrated and you think, "I'll never do this again," and "I need to find another job". You go to the supermarket and you think: "God, wouldn't it be nice to be sitting there at the check-out." (laughs) That's how you think, and I'm not the only one. I've heard the same from others too. And then, suddenly, everything starts to work out again, and you're over the moon. But it really eats you up inside when it's not working out.

Another says:

> I think it goes in waves between feeling really pleased with myself (small laugh) and feeling really doubtful about whether I am able to get to the end of this at all.

A third says:

> I've never felt so manic-depressive in my whole life.

The strength of the emotional rollercoaster effect is probably amplified by the way research is organised, especially within the humanities and social sciences. As one PhD fellow says:

---

2   See also Jacobsen (2001a) for a description of research as resistance.

3   Excerpts from interviews are presented in a manner that protects the anonymity of interviewees. Implicit meanings and references to place names and names of persons are indicated in square brackets. Non-verbal expressions, called vocalisations, such as laughter, sighs, etc. are indicated in round brackets when they are deemed to influence the reader's interpretation of the excerpt. Non-verbal features that are interwoven in the verbal text, e.g. stuttered speech, condensed speech, etc. are indicated in brackets before the text sequence at issue, for example (stuttered), but are only included to the extent that these features are explicit elements of the interpretation in question. Likewise, 'um', 'ah' and filler words are only included when they contribute to the interpretation of an excerpt, the presentation being designed to ensure readability. This also entails that some excerpts are spliced together from two parts of a given interview. Excerpts that have been spliced together are indicated by the insertion of three dots (...)

I think that everyone who is new to the labour market feels that many demands are made on them. Most people [here] are busy, and frustrated that they can't get as much done as they would like to. But the biggest difference [between the labour market and Academia] as I see it, is that you spend so much time on your own, and that's why your [emotional] ups and downs are more pronounced in both directions. Everything is just so much more uncertain.

Another PhD fellow says:

You're so isolated... if you had an ordinary job and worked with some ordinary people in an ordinary environment, then at some point you'd have been told, "Hey, that was a bloody good bit of work you did there", or "Hey, that was really crap." Here, you are wrapped up inside your own little cocoon, without a clue about what's going on out there. So you have to find some means of keeping yourself going.

The PhD fellow is alone with her project. Is she on the right track? Is the work on schedule? What are the demands? As one of them says:

I think frustration best describes the feeling that's talked about with the other PhD students. Many of them are frustrated that it's hard to get things done in time. It's virtually impossible, and everyone knows it's impossible, but they still want to get there. It's especially frustrating because you don't really know what the demands are, and there isn't really anybody who is willing to tell you. They [the supervisors] like to add on an extra 50 per cent for safety's sake, so they are sure they haven't demanded too little.

Recent studies of the emotions of research emphasise such feelings as curiosity, nervous curiosity, feeling responsible, uncertain, happy about making discoveries, and the feeling of involvement, which is the basis for the insistent stubbornness needed for pursuing research (Barbalet 2002, Arber 1954, Ehn and Löfgren 2004). These PhD fellows also highlight a number of other emotions such as doubt, frustration and hopelessness. Furthermore, their narratives illustrate ways in which phases of the research process are interwoven with emotional fluctuations that involve the person's self-esteem. Research is a manic-depressive activity that swings between melancholic phases and explosions of creativity, between 'getting stuck' and 'breaking free' (Ehn and Löfgren 2004: 84). The PhD fellow must learn to manage all of these emotions.

Self-esteem, belief and trust are not only dependent on the activity of doing research, but also on the comments and assessments of the PhD fellow's project offered by supervisors and other members of staff, for example at research seminars. Every scientific choice is also a political investment strategy with a view to gaining recognition from colleagues, as well as influence (Bourdieu 1975). The PhD fellow's project can thus be used as a weapon in academic disputes about correct science and appropriate paradigms.

PhD fellows, being at the bottom of the academic hierarchy, do not have a status shield to protect them against random attacks and abuse.[4] This position makes them particularly exposed to demonstrations of power and status that can undermine their self-esteem. Kemper (1978a) has developed a theory regarding the relationship between emotions and displays of power and status as experienced. This theory also draws a distinction between whether one perceives oneself or the other person as being responsible for a given display of this kind. Kemper's theory is employed in the following analysis as a tool that serves to highlight some of the emotional processes that arise from the PhD fellows' position in the hierarchical structure.[5]

Emotions of the Supervisor Relationship

All PhD fellows are assigned a supervisor. The supervisor can be seen as the PhD fellow's lifeline to Academia. Previously, within some fields this relationship resembled that of an apprentice and master, the PhD student following and participating in the supervisor's research. Today, the supervisor's role more closely resembles that of a coach or sparring partner. The PhD fellow and the supervisor typically have their own independent research projects, and the relationship can be defined as that of a 'supervised thesis' (Jacobsen 2001a: 78).[6] This relationship is not purely based upon sparring, however. Since the supervisor has the power to end a fellowship prematurely, the relationship is subject to ongoing negotiation.

A study undertaken by Hanne Nexø Jensen (2000) documents that three out of four PhD fellows are satisfied with their supervisors. But what is a satisfactory relationship to one's supervisor? One woman describes her good relationship with her supervisor in the following way:

> It's really important to have a supervisor who shares your understanding of science and of what makes the world go round. This is absolutely vital, because

---

4   For further elucidation of the concept of status shield, see Hochschild 2003: 136.

5   According to Kemper (1978a), any social relationship can be characterised in terms of experienced power and status relations. The power dimension refers to resources and actions by means of which one can enforce one's will, while the status dimension refers to the accordance of recognition, respect, friendliness, sympathy or their opposites. Kemper's point thereafter is that different power and status relations evoke specific emotions. Kemper distinguishes three types of emotions: 1) 'structural' emotions, which are emotions based on a stable power and status relation (also called a power and a status structure); 2) 'anticipatory' emotions, which refer to expectations regarding a given relationship. These emotions are based on previous experience, resources and conditions; 3) 'consequence' emotions, which are situational emotions based on the interplay between anticipatory and structural emotions. My empirical material does not provide a basis for including all of these distinctions in my analysis.

6   Elements of apprenticeship still exist in some fields.

once that's in place you can really get something out of it. And if that's not in place, you spend ten times more energy arguing with the person. It's also incredibly important to have the kind of relationship in which you feel that you can give each other feedback that is positive, and you can be confident that if the supervisor says something like, "Listen here now, you have to – you really have to do something about this," then you really listen and take it on board. I mean, my supervisor – I have a really good relationship with her – and if she says something like, "Now, you pull yourself together," in some area or other and make improvements, then I'll certainly do just that, because I trust her judgement. Yes, and I know on some level that she's on my side. That's so important, because then you take in what the other person is saying, don't you?

This PhD student is describing a relationship in which the supervisor is perceived as an authority, but the relationship is also based on mutual professional respect and interpersonal trust and understanding. She is satisfied with this relationship, and a relationship of this kind gives rise to feelings of security, pleasure and self-esteem. However, a supervisor and PhD fellow can also be working within different scientific paradigms and do not therefore share their assessments of the PhD fellow's project. Academic differences can be negotiated with mutual respect for professional points of view, or the supervisor can choose to threaten the PhD fellow. Here is an example of the kind of interaction, in which the PhD fellow experiences the supervisor as playing a power game and also feels that her own status is being denigrated by her supervisor.

I presented my thoughts to my supervisor, but the way she spoke to me... She was patronising, virtually threatening, and I felt that what really affronted her was the fact that I hadn't referred to her work or used it as my point of departure. I've given a lot of thought to this. I don't want to continue with her any more, because I don't feel that she understands my approach, and I can't bear the way she talks to me.

Displays of power provoke fear and anxiety, while behaviour that is perceived as denigrating one's status triggers hopelessness and depressive feelings. When the other party in an interaction is perceived as the agent of such displays, however, these feelings are extrojected as feelings of anger and hostility. In this example, the PhD fellow does not describe anxiety and fear, but rather strong and persistent feelings of humiliation and anger in relation to her supervisor.[7] These feelings indicate that this PhD fellow does not see fault on her own part as having given rise to the behaviour of her supervisor. Blame is rather accorded to the supervisor.

---

7 Suspicion of supervisors' academic intentions is also expressed as distrust, fear of intellectual theft and exploitation of the PhD fellows' work. Such ideas were widespread among PhD fellows in Gerholm and Gerholm's study (1991).

In the following example, another PhD fellow does seem to have accepted her own inadequacies as having precipitated the negative reactions of her supervisor:

> As a student, one is so dependent on one's supervisor. I also have one good and one evil supervisor. I've been in to the evil one and cried my eyes out,[8] because I thought that things had simply gone far enough, and I just wanted to tell him a thing or two. So then I was informed about what the hierarchy was exactly: professor, associate professor and at the bottom, me, the PhD fellow. I've also been informed in writing: "You do not have what it takes, but you're welcome to surprise me." I felt just so … like you said, just so helpless. And I was raging mad about the fact that he wouldn't arrange a meeting with me, because he said I had to do certain things first. So every time I said, "Do you have time to meet to talk about it?" – he didn't have time. On the other hand, he could just bang open my door and say I had to do this or that, and now they would send me a formal letter, and then it comes: "You do not have what it takes [to write a PhD thesis], but you can try to surprise us." You're enormously dependent on a person like that because he's such an authority, and I really wanted to hear his comments. I was at the point that every time I turned on my computer, I always thought, "No, probably I don't have what it takes." For a long time it was really hard, struggling against that. When someone else has power over you, that's when you feel really helpless, isn't it?

We are not in a position to judge whether this supervisor's threatened termination of this PhD fellowship was academically reasonable and well-founded. It is clear, however, that the PhD fellow feels threatened by this display of power and that she experiences a marked loss of status. Experiences of this kind give rise to fear and anxiety, as well as hopelessness and depression. Fear and anxiety are hinted at in this excerpt, and later in the interview she describes how she subsequently felt both helpless and depressed.[9] These emotions indicate that to a great extent this PhD fellow takes her own inadequacies as having given rise to the supervisor's comments and reactions. In the next example, a man talks about his supervisor:

> He [the supervisor] is rude and offensive, ignores and neglects you, and treats you like dirt. He says things like, "I don't care what you have to say" – and that's before you've even said anything at all. He just brushes you off, you know? … Like, he just calls me in to complain about this project – that it wasn't really on

---

8   Several of the PhD fellows made a distinction between their good and evil supervisors. The evil supervisor was perceived as an academic authority, but also as a person that did not show respect for other human beings. The good supervisor was perceived as kind and supportive, but often without academic authority.

9   According to Kemper's theory, if this PhD student had solely blamed the supervisor for the character of their relationship, her depressed feelings would have been transformed into anger and hostility (Kemper 1978a: 60-63).

track or on schedule. That is actually his fault, because he hadn't been keeping an eye on things [in the laboratory] – checking what was happening and that nothing was wrong. So then, oh, he reads the riot act and then he says, "This... has got to be fixed, right now." He didn't care the slightest bit about me – I'd have to work 90 hours a week. At our lab we already work our butts off, so to get this sorted we would have to put in 90 hours instead of 60. He didn't care about that. It just had to be dealt with, and ASAP. There was no question of scheduling it for the week ahead or anything like that. It had to be done right there and then.

The interviewer asks what he feels in this situation, and he answers:

IP:(thinking aloud) I… feel powerless, a little bit sad, but that has become less so because one learns to cope with it. You also feel irritated and think, "What the hell."

I:[10] Angry?

IP: No, I feel more hurt than angry.

This PhD fellow experiences a display of power and status denigration by the supervisor. Displays of power provoke fear and anxiety, and he describes a feeling of powerlessness, but also irritation. The irritation indicates that he sees the supervisor as the person responsible for this display of power. He also describes how he feels sad and hurt. These emotions arise from the denigration of his status and his emotional reaction indicates that on this point he accepts the blame.

Displays of power and status denigration often occur together, but the PhD fellows also describe pure status denigrating displays on the part of their supervisors. One of them says the following:

For some time I had a rather weird relationship with one of my supervisors because he didn't show up for the meetings we'd arranged. I built up a lot of anger about this over several months. Well, I'm not sure that it's only anger, it's also a feeling of powerlessness… he doesn't come and talk to me when we've agreed to meet. I spend a lot of time and energy on handing in working papers, and then he just doesn't show up. It's like getting a slap in the face. Then, the day before yesterday – I must say, I don't usually react like this – but I just lost it completely. Because I'd been sitting waiting from around one o'clock until four thirty, and he still hadn't appeared. So I went down and had a word with one of my other supervisors, who hadn't seen him either. He [the other supervisor] could see I was fairly put out, and then he said, "Come in and talk to me". As soon as I'd shut the door, I just broke down and burst into tears. Well, it

---

10 Some excerpts are presented as dialogue between interviewer and interviewee. 'I' is an abbreviation of 'interviewer', while 'IP' is an abbreviation of 'interviewed person'.

was so embarrassing, because I'm usually pretty hardcore, you know? "I've got everything under control" – kind of thing. I was so, totally hysterical. He just sat there and stared at me in amazement. Even now, two days later, I still feel really frail. It wouldn't take much to make me burst into tears again.

The supervisor 'forgets the PhD fellow' and she experiences this treatment as a 'slap in the face'. This status denigration, which is apparently just one incident among many, triggers strong feelings that are so overwhelming that she loses control and starts to cry in public. Many feelings – anger, sorrow, etc. – can make a person weep, but her description of how she still feels 'really frail' indicates that she directs these feelings inwards towards herself rather than outwards in the form of anger and hostility towards her supervisor.

The supervisor relationship is the lifeline of the PhD fellow. Fruitful cooperation between a supervisor and a PhD fellow is the key to a successful thesis (Molin and Åsells 1996). Most PhD fellows are satisfied with their supervisors (Jensen 2000). In a study undertaken by Appel (2003), however, 67 per cent of the women and 56 per cent of the men state problems with their supervisor as the reason for considering giving up a PhD. The supervisor relationship is important, not only because it provides a context for sparring, but also because it is a relationship in which power is unequally distributed and only one of the participants is protected by a shield of status. In this light, it is worth noting that the majority of the PhD fellows in Appel's study state that they are afraid to bring up problems because they are afraid of provoking the supervisor's censure. Is this a question of fearing displays of power and status denigration on the part of the supervisor?

Emotions of the Power Structure

Ongoing academic battles between different groups are a feature of Academia. Since PhD fellows have neither power advantages nor status shields, their research projects can be used with relatively little cost to highlight battle fronts and demarcation lines between various groups of academics. The following excerpts illustrate the ways in which a PhD fellow's project can be used as a weapon in a power game between colleagues:

> I once attended a PhD course where an [external] associate professor [name] was one of the opponents. I presented a particular theory that I wanted to use in my PhD project, but then, [name] said, "You can't just use that theory in isolation. You have to study everything that author has written, you have to know his philosophy and so on." Well, I felt really awful for weeks afterwards. I felt this meant that now I wouldn't be able to write about this. So, I'd have to drop it because I just couldn't, I couldn't face having to read all that, I couldn't do it.

The interviewer asks what she had done in that situation, and she answers:

Yes, what did I say? Yes, I think, I was very silent (laughs). I'm not the type that sticks to my guns, not yet anyway, and says, "And now, I would like to present my defence!" But it was right at the start [of my PhD], so I was very humble and overawed.

An external associate professor uses this research project to underline an academic hierarchy between the associate professor's own department, which is very theory-oriented, and the PhD fellow's department, which is less strong on theory. This is achieved by means of presenting academic criticism of the PhD fellow's project. The PhD fellow feels academically threatened and humiliated, and her subsequent reactions (giving up and loosing confidence) indicate that she perceives the criticism as justified. It is only much later that she realises that her project was being used in a power game between colleagues. Here is another example:

> I presented my project at one of those meetings, at which people tell a bit about what they are doing in the department. There was this permanent member of staff sitting in the corner, who made disdainful remarks and laughed at the wrong times. He also laughed at our professor, who is my supervisor, and who had asked some interested questions. The fellow in the corner also made disdainful remarks to him. That made me angry, but I didn't really show how I felt.

A colleague of his supervisor thus uses the PhD fellow's project to criticise the supervisor and his academic approach. This is done by poking fun at and making disdainful remarks about the PhD fellow's project, that is, by means of a display of power and status denigration. According to Kemper's theory, such displays provoke fear and sadness, but insofar as these feelings are perceived as being caused by the other person, they are transformed into anger. The PhD fellow becomes angry, and his account also indicates that he does not attribute blame to himself.

Finally, here is an almost humorous account of how a PhD fellow's project can be used as the point of departure for academic demarcations and battles between associate and full professors. The situation described by this woman concerns the mid-term evaluation of her PhD project:

> I had made a presentation that focused on my empirical results, and then they fell over each other to criticise me. But they didn't really pull my project apart. They all believed that my project was about something in particular, and what they thought it was about, was very close to what they were doing themselves. So, they all read me into their own stuff without trying to find out where I stood. After the break they really got going – it was the leading six or seven 55-year-old men in the room – they got dug into a pissing contest about what I was doing. One of them believed that I was really engaged in a study that resembled work found in [name]'s research, and that I ought to include more [author name] in order to understand more about Danish intellectual life. Another one believed that my project was based on systems theory, and that I ought to draw more

> on early American colonial history. A third one said I should use more of the postmodernists. Yes, and I should draw more on Deleuze, and a fourth said I should use more Niclas Luhman, and so on. It just kept on, and not one of them asked me what I thought. Nobody addressed their remarks to me, and nobody said, "The material you have presented is interesting," or anything like that. So, I felt it was like being at a Wimbledon match, when the spectators' heads turn first one way, and then the other. I just sat watching the ball being hit back and forth on my court, you know what I mean? They were just pissing out their territory. Not that I was being asked to join in, they were just pissing the other gorillas off the court. I wasn't part of it at all. I was left on the sideline, watching the big males battle it out. The one that wins would take over, automatically.

These 'big males' do not threaten her project, they simply ignore it. This PhD fellow does not say what she feels in this situation, but the interview as a whole reveals subsequent reactions of fear and anxiety in relation to both assistant and associate professors.[11]

In the same way as the analysis of the supervisor relationship, these examples illustrate how the PhD fellows' position at the bottom of the academic hierarchy creates the conditions for displays of power and status that provoke feelings in PhD fellows that undermine their belief and confidence in their own abilities and in their research projects.

Segmentation of Emotions

> If one sees a PhD thesis as an emotional journey during which people are picked or rejected according to who makes it through the survival course and who doesn't, then it is clear that what one needs to do is to re-arm oneself emotionally. It is a huge emotional challenge. It really helps if one is aware of that.

Doing a PhD involves processes of socialisation and selection, during which the PhD fellow must learn to handle his or her emotions in accordance with the given academic emotional culture. Emotions are immediate dispositions to act (fear makes us take flight from the situation; anger leads to counterattack, and so on). These dispositions must be diverted, adapted and transformed in order to accord with the given feeling rules and power structure. In the excerpt above, a woman describes the need to 'emotionally re-arm' herself in order to complete her PhD. In the sociology of emotions, this form of rearmament is termed emotion work. PhD fellows process their emotions in private, but they also do so together. The

---

11 See also Henriksson et al. (2000) for an analysis of research seminars. Henriksson et al. distinguish between the manifest content of seminars, which comprises a constructive exchange of opinions and assessments, and the latent content, which is primarily a fight for position.

Danish sociologist Poul Poder (2004) has introduced the concept of 'segmented emotion work'. Segmentation refers to ways in which the same emotion is processed, handled and expressed differently in different contexts. Segmentation is thus a spatial concept, which refers to the selection of appropriate expressions of emotion according to whether a particular social situation calls for strategic considerations or is one characterised by mutual trust. It transpires that these PhD fellows handle their emotions within several different contexts: the private space, the academic space and the collective space. The latter includes only PhDs and excludes members of staff more highly placed in the academic hierarchy. Whether this space develops in the form of a community depends of course on the number of PhD fellows in a given setting. This prerequisite, combined with the condition of being newcomers and located at the bottom of the hierarchy, creates the basis for the development of a community.

The Private Space

The PhD fellow uses a variety of techniques to process and transform specific feelings in private.[12]

The doubts and uncertainties associated with research as an activity are stressful and present a challenge to the PhD fellow's self-confidence as a researcher. In addition, as the next chapter will show, feelings of this kind do not accord with the norms of academic emotional culture. Therefore, as one PhD fellow expresses the problem: you have to find 'some means of keeping yourself going'. In the interviews, the PhD fellows primarily describe cognitive techniques by means of which they seek to modify negative self-esteem. One such technique is that of evoking positive images in order to convince themselves that they can in fact cope. As a PhD fellow says:

> One can sit there reproaching oneself and saying, "Am I really good enough to do this?" – even though one knows very well of course that in many areas one is, yes, one is bloody-well good enough... I've had that feeling loads of times (laughs).

The PhD fellows' narratives also illustrate how they seek to modify negative feelings towards their supervisors by focusing on positive feelings regarding their good sides, such as their expertise and the nicer aspects of their temperaments. For example, after describing how his supervisor had verbally attacked him, one PhD fellow says:

---

12 Feelings are managed when we try to evoke, suppress or modify them. In connection with modifying endeavours, Hochschild distinguishes between three techniques: a cognitive technique, whereby we change the images and ideas associated with the emotion; a physical technique, whereby we try to change the bodily expression of an emotion, and an expressive technique, whereby we change our outer expression and thereby the emotion (2003).

> Well, it's not that you should let yourself be scared out of your wits [by the supervisor's overbearing behaviour], because he's also a really nice person – and he's a happy guy. He can be extremely euphoric, and he really is clever. And then, you also have to remember that you are dependent on him. If he were just some ordinary guy, he wouldn't be able to get away with it. But because he is so bright and I can get so much out of him now – and maybe also in ten years' time – it's important that I keep dancing to his tune. So, sometimes he really has a lot to offer, and then there are times when he just gives you a bashing.

The supervisor's positive sides are used to neutralise the felt anger, while the supervisor's professional expertise is used as a defence for continuing under his supervision on the basis of strategic considerations. One PhD fellow has this response to a suggestion that he should find a different supervisor:

> No, I can't [find another supervisor], because he's such a genius. I don't want to get rid of him. I couldn't do this research project without him. Well, maybe I could, but then it wouldn't be just as good.

By means of cognitive emotion work the PhD fellows seek to modify negative self-feelings and negative feelings towards people higher up in the hierarchy. Some also seek to boost their self-esteem by trying to handle the emotions of others.[13] One PhD fellow reports:

> I have been very conscious of the way in which I present my own project – because the news that you are not competent spreads very quickly, if your supervisor is negative about it. So I have made a point of saying to others, "I'll make the deadline, and I've accomplished this and this and this." And I've passed on that advice to some of the others. Funnily enough I passed it on to two other girls who have been a bit uncertain about their own projects, couldn't get them completed and had some problems. So, I said to them, "Everything that you say about your project from now on must only be positive. You've written so many chapters, you've made progress with the theoretical part, and you've done this and you've done that." I heard back from one of them the other day and she said that it really works – because the word spreads very quickly here about whether people are confident or whether they're trying to disappear into the walls. You mustn't say anything negative about your project or voice your uncertainty. You mustn't advertise your uncertainty. You must at least make sure that you don't hand out the ammunition that will be used to undermine you in here. It's a deliberate strategy, but I'm not sure whether it works or not.

---

13 For a more detailed analysis of handling others' emotions, see Thoits (1996, 2004).

The Academic Space

The PhD fellows describe many feelings in their encounters with supervisors, opponents, professors, etc. Generally, however, they try not to show their feelings or to provoke feelings among staff members higher up in the hierarchy. Why is this? The PhD fellows themselves claim that this is due to the power structure. They are dependent on the permanent members of staff for supervision, grants and continued employment, such that the safest strategy is to hide their feelings and otherwise remain neutral in any conflicts between permanent staff members. As one PhD fellow says:

> My professor is on half of all the important committees and apart from that, he knows all the others. You never know whether one of them will say something, whether they'll dish the dirt on you beforehand. But at any rate I want to make sure they don't, so I just keep a neutral position.

She continues:

> They have your job in their hands and I don't want to spoil my chances, as I think it's incredibly hard to find a job. I've spent so much time applying for lots of jobs, so I need to stay on the good side of as many people as possible – if I can. This is simply because I haven't got very far yet and don't have any position at all.

Neutrality is perceived as the least dangerous course in terms of maintaining beneficial relationships.

> If there is trouble brewing between the professor and my supervisor I stay well clear so I'm not asked to take a position on anything. I don't want to say something to one of them about the other, even though I may well have an opinion about their conflict. It's often a question of doing a particular experiment or not; getting samples from it or not. We PhDs do have opinions, and we usually end up doing the work. I really try to steer clear of that. I just don't get involved … Strategically it's best to be just like a fly on the wall … but then again, maybe they would respect you more if you had an opinion, but I actually would rather not have any opinion about that kind of thing. I'd rather just get back to my laboratory and stay there. That's the way we play the game.

This PhD fellow does not want to risk conflict with anyone higher up in the hierarchy, but some also feel that they do not have the authority to become engaged in academic disputes.

> I think it has a lot to do with the fact that you don't feel you have enough authority to contribute. So, again, it's some kind of feeling of inferiority. You think that you probably won't be taken seriously – that you are just a PhD

student. If I get a job one day or something like that (laughs a lot) I'll have a lot more ballast – be a lot more qualified – to stand up and put up a good fight. But that's not something I dare to do as a PhD student.

PhD fellows try to present themselves as being emotionally neutral within the academic space, or, as one of them put it 'like a fly on the wall'. This also means that problematic relationships, which could give rise to anger, fear or shame, are kept concealed. On this point, one PhD fellow says:

> I'm on the PhD study council and we discuss the fact that although many PhDs are never completed, almost nobody lodges a complaint. I think the main reason is that people don't want to fall out with their supervisors, because often they're on all kinds of committees that will be making decisions about grants. But if you don't get on with your supervisor this might very well be because the supervisor is simply not good enough, mightn't it? There's a lot of talk at the moment about finding some way or other to disqualify supervisors and then actively following up on all the PhDs that were never completed. It's a big problem. I think it's a really big problem.

According to the study by Appel (2000), a majority of PhD fellows refrain from bringing up problems because they fear the supervisor's dissatisfaction. This excerpt presents the same issue. PhD fellows refrain from complaining about problems in fear of 'falling out' with the supervisor. But why is this dangerous? These PhD fellows suggest that the answer lies in power relations and the distribution of resources. This is why they do not make their voices heard. It can also be mentioned that six out of ten PhD fellows in Appel's study did not believe that their departments handled conflicts appropriately.

The Collective Space

PhD fellows share a number of circumstances that can provide the basis for a PhD community. The character of this community can vary between departments. In the health sciences, there are usually many PhDs who work together directly in laboratories. In the humanities, in contrast, PhDs more often work alone on their own projects in their own offices. The PhD community functions as a space in which to vent feelings and frustrations about research, supervisors and the department as such. The PhD community is an important space for collective emotion work and especially for recognising that one is not alone with particular feelings. The following excerpts illustrate some of the ways in which the emotions of research are processed within PhD communities:

> For more than half a year I had a project that wasn't working out. I was doing it with someone else, so we were able to back each other up a bit. But it nearly finished both of us, you know?

> But you don't [break down in frustration due to all the challenges of doing research], because you have all the others around you... I talk to everyone in the laboratory, both the technicians and the other PhDs.

> People talk openly about popping a tranquilliser or about the pressure they're under. During coffee breaks in the kitchen, there's a lot of talk about how people are feeling. We often talk about it... We are a big group in our department, both men and women, who talk about how they feel when they're down in the dumps or up in the air. There are a few who don't share their feelings, but a lot do.

The PhD fellows discuss the emotions that arise when doing research, and they talk over the power structure together. The following examples illustrate how PhD fellows relate collectively to status denigrating strategies on the part of professors or supervisors:

> If the professor has been mad at one of us, we're all there straight away to give our support.

The PhD fellows back each other up, and they may also discuss how to tackle a professor's unreasonable behaviour more offensively.

> We discuss how we need to have a defence strategy ready the next time we're attacked – for example, that we have initiated these five things [experiments, measurements, etc.] or whatever. That's one side of it. The other is that we warn each other – one goes out and tells the others that he's being a real bastard today.

Other PhD fellows describe how they together develop a collective distance and an ironic approach to the power struggles they witness:

> There's a lot of nepotism and small agreements made on the quiet and all that stuff that wears some people down. As a PhD, I've an in-between status – neither a real teacher nor a student. There are a lot of quiet agreements about appointments and so on, but, yes, we try to keep an ironic distance to it all. We know it goes on, but we think we deal with it in a fairly reasonable way (laughs).

> Of course we have our views about the stuff that goes on, and I've sometimes gone out for a coffee with some of my colleagues and had a good gossip about it all – chatted about how some associate professor or other is a waste of space (laughs). So in that way it's possible to have these hidden fora, where you can air your views about the goings on in the department (smiles).

Finally, academic 'counter-groups' are formed as a collective way of coping with the conditions of PhD life. One PhD fellow says the following:

I've got together with some of my colleagues to discuss our concept of science – how feelings can be involved in doing research, and how it can be an advantage rather than a drawback to be emotionally involved in one's field. In this group we have laughed a lot because… (laughs). We've had some rather peculiar discussions (laughs), we've discussed the assumption that you shouldn't be emotionally involved in your field, because then it's not real research. But we all have fields we have chosen because we are emotionally involved in them, and we want to hang on to that, even though some of the old ones [associate and full professors] criticise us for being involved. We have set up a discussion group on that basis, and I must say it has been great fun and we have had a lot of laughs (laughs)… We're a special group, since we've picked each other out as people working in fields that we're involved in. I think things like that are great to do because they give you something… I mean, it's great, because then you're not so affected by quite different reactions in other situations… It gives you something to hang on to.

Solidarity and Competition

PhD fellows experience solidarity in their relationships with each other, using each other for collective emotion work, while also being competitors in terms of their ongoing academic careers. One PhD fellow expresses this tension between solidarity and competition as follows:

On the surface, it doesn't seem to be a problem – everything is going to be ok, and you never make negative comments about one another's work. Yet, it's quite clear at the same time that some people have a lot more going for them than others, and everyone also knows that it's tougher for some people than for others.

This describes the tension between solidarity and competition in neutral terms. Other PhD fellows describe this tension in more emotionally laden ways. For example, one says:

We are a project group of eight people, who are incredibly good at supporting each other and always really happy when something goes well for one of us. Even though, deep down, we are competitors – just as we are in the department – but we're still a large group of people that's very good at showing spontaneous delight about something or other. It's a really nice feeling.

Another PhD fellow comments on this as follows: 'Well then, you're really lucky – the competition at our place is tougher.' A third adds this comment:

There's also an element of one-upmanship. I've written for [a magazine] a few times and probably published more articles than many of my co-students. But I know that isn't something you sit and brag about at lunch. You have to keep a low profile about things like that. You can't let yourself be spontaneously happy in Academia. You have to take some account of other people's situations the whole time.

This excerpt indicates a feeling norm regarding the need to not show spontaneous delight about one's own success. It also illustrates the delicate balance between solidarity and competition. This entails that even though one can express frustration about one's thesis, supervisor, etc. to other PhD students, there are nevertheless limits to how open one can be about academic failures and fiascos. As one PhD fellow says:

> I prefer to forget about embarrassing things. It's not because we laugh at each other, but I do think they [other PhD fellows] don't have to know everything. I wouldn't want to seem to be the dumbest PhD student in the department. Rationally speaking, I don't believe they would think I was. But one just doesn't want to be [seen as stupid]. Then you'd be the one that's whispered about in the corners – like, "Yes, [name] we should never have taken her on. What will become of her?" I don't want to end up like that. I do some of the whispering myself, about this or that and all the stories about one person or another that crop up. So, I'm well aware that if I really mess up they'll whisper about me too. I can do without that, at any rate being the one that 'doesn't think twice about what she's doing'. That's not me at all.

The category 'stupid' is a central category of assessment in the everyday language of academia. Being stupid is the worst thing possible (Hasse 2003), so academic failures and fiascos that might incur this assessment are kept hidden.

The PhD community has its limitations. It is a fellowship of feelings, but when it comes to academic positioning, solidarity can be relegated to the background while the presentation of the academic self moves into the foreground. As one PhD fellow says:

> We get on well together socially, at parties and so on. We have a great time, playing guitar and doing all sorts of things. But once it comes to academic matters, we all take on a different kind of mask. Then, as I see it, one tries to show a lot more discretion.

Summary

PhD fellows are located at the bottom of the academic hierarchy. This position provides the basis for a number of emotions. I have used Kemper's theory to highlight some of these, and to assess whether PhD students perceive the use of power threats and status denigration as being due to their own inadequacies or as being due to the person of the supervisor, the use of academic power games and so on.

The heading of this chapter indicates the emotional challenge involved in completing a PhD, a view that is confirmed by these PhD fellows. Compared to other status groups in Academia, the emotion work undertaken by PhD fellows takes a special form, which I have illustrated by using the concept of 'segmented emotion work'. Emotion work entails that one seeks to match one's feelings to the prevailing feeling norms. This is not to imply that this attempt is always successful. Segmented emotion work does not guarantee positive self-esteem, belief in one's project and in the academic organisation. The survey of Swedish PhD fellows undertaken by Appel (2000, 2003) documents that more than half of them often experience stress and mental exhaustion, and also that every fourth woman and every fifth man, based on their experiences, would not have started a PhD if they had known what it entailed. The process of completing a PhD is also a process of selection. The Swedish ethnographer Fredrik Schoug shows how PhDs gradually become polarised into two groups: so-called internalists and externalists.[14] Internalism comprises a complex of attitudes that includes belief and trust in the values of Academia, pure research, the notion of excellence, meritocracy, etc., while externalism comprises a complex of attitudes defined by distrusting the values of Academia, the ideology of competition and meritocracy, in favour of orienting oneself towards the external social world. Those PhD fellows who have completed or are close to completing their theses usually favour internalism. Those who are relative losers in the competition for resources are more likely to favour externalism. Their self-confidence and belief in their research projects are frail, and they express critical attitudes towards the values and conventions of Academia and its competitive ideology.[15]

Different organisations communicate and maintain their emotional culture by means of ceremonies, targeted supervision of newcomers and selective recruitment of longer term members (Maanen and Kunda 1989). Completing a PhD thesis can be conceived as part of a prolonged recruitment process, which is designed to secure members that also can be relied upon to act in accordance with the emotional culture of Academia.

These PhD fellows attempt to hide their feelings from the world outside their own community and to display affective neutrality, remaining 'a fly on the wall'.

---

14 Schoug's work (2002, 2003, 2004) is based on an interview study of 68 Swedish PhD fellows and researchers who had recently defended their theses.

15 As previously mentioned, PhD fellows are exposed to a process of selection regarding future careers in research. In this respect, the survey of PhD fellows' career paths undertaken by Hanne Nexø Jensen is interesting. This study shows that PhD fellows adapt their expectations to the future, such that it is primarily university-funded fellows who expect further employment at the university, while sector-financed and privately-financed PhD fellows do not have these expectations. Rather, they are oriented towards sector research and private industry. Hanne Nexø Jensen does not study their attitudes to Academia as such, but the expectations identified may reflect tacit selection processes and related attitudes.

The emotional culture of Academia, however, entails more than being a fly on the wall. In the competition for 'survival of the fittest', a prerequisite for success is the ability to present oneself in ways that contribute to advancement and visibility in the academic world. Some of these strategies were particularly clearly described by assistant professors, who have their say in the next chapter.

Chapter 4
The Order of Visibility

Academic life involves a multiplicity of unwritten rules. There are rules regarding the presentation of research, the use of equipment and software, the norms of academic writing and the use of footnotes, as well as rules of conversation in a variety of contexts. There are also numerous unspoken rules regarding desirable conduct and the presentation of self that must be observed, if recognition and a successful academic career are to be achieved.

In a survey among assistant professors regarding their perception of criteria for gaining recognition at their workplaces, academic excellence was emphasised as the key criterion, but many also emphasised the importance of moral, emotional and behavioural criteria. There were requirements to be friendly, sociable and supportive, not to criticise, boast or be openly ambitious, not to show signs of weakness, and to hide one's personal life (Bloch and Dalsgård 2002c).[1]

These prescriptions and proscriptions can be interpreted as ideal feeling rules and rules of expression. Nevertheless, we do not always feel the way we would want to – or ought to – feel.

This chapter aims to present examples of the strategic handling of emotions in Academia that is undertaken with a view to achieving recognition. These strategies, which I term *'the politics of friendliness'*, 'the *deceiving game' and 'ventriloquism',* belong to the tacit emotional culture of Academia. All of the interviewees were familiar with these strategies and some, but not all, use them successfully. They are described in most detail by the assistant professor group.

The Politics of Friendliness

In Academia, it is necessary to be friendly, sociable and flexible. Friendliness as a feeling rule entails that one generally endeavours to maintain a polite and well-mannered tone in every social exchange. Friendliness also has a strategic dimension, however. Since colleagues assess each other, it can be desirable to maintain friendly relationships with one's potential assessors.

---

1 The empirical material for this study is based on Hanne Nexø Jensen's survey of assistant professors, specifically on responses to the following two open questions: 'What leads to recognition in your everyday working environment?' and 'What gives rise to disapproval in your everyday working environment?' The quantitative analysis showed that most respondents stated academic excellence as the criterion for according recognition, but two thirds of respondents also emphasised other criteria concerning conduct and feeling rules.

In career terms, an assistant professor is a provisional winner. The appointment is nevertheless a period of probation, during which he or she has to prove academic worth and also secure good relationships with those who can promote a future academic career.[2] This special position may be the reason why assistant professors particularly emphasise friendliness as a necessary political strategy. One assistant professor puts it this way:

> Well, it's necessary to be able to work with others. So, sometimes you have to put anger aside and just ... well, say, "OK, we'll do it that way." If they've all been doing it that way, I guess I'd better do the same. It's a kind of strategic taming [of emotions], when I can see that I probably shouldn't make a fuss. After all, I'm still only an assistant professor and in principle I'm still on trial. I should probably wait before starting to get their backs up – both socially, with colleagues, and academically too. It would be really stupid to spend my time as an assistant professor getting into the bad books of various faculty members – or cleaning personnel and administrative staff for that matter.

The assistant professor describes a 'strategic taming' of emotions. This may entail emotion work with a view to modifying one's feelings, but it may also take the form of just pretending to have friendly feelings that one does not have. The latter can give rise to moral scruples and thereby to new feelings that have to be handled (Ashfort and Tomiuk 2000). On this point, one man, also an assistant professor has this to say:

> When you hear an associate professor arriving in the morning in a rotten mood and biting the head off a lab technician, who usually does a really good job, just because this associate professor has some personal problems or got out of the wrong side of the bed, and you don't intervene and say something ... You may have heard this kind of thing countless times before, but you still don't say anything. Because you want to keep things ticking along – because if you were to interfere, it might backfire on you later. One simply doesn't want a conflict

---

2 Like PhD fellows, assistant professors at Danish institutions of higher education are appointed for a three-year period. Assistant professors, who wish to continue as associate professors at the same institution must apply for that position and compete on an equal footing with other qualified candidates. In formal terms, assistant professors are assessed on the basis of their academic and pedagogical qualifications. Other criteria that may be employed by the assessment committee – such as cooperation skills, personal commitment or departmental policy regarding academic priorities, finances and resource-related considerations – are unknown. A three-year assistant professorship can thus be seen as one long probationary period, on insecure terms. Compared to other western countries, a Danish assistant professorship is held for a relatively short period of time. Moreover, an assistant professor cannot apply for promotion on the basis of his or her qualifications, but must wait for the department to announce an associate professorship, which the assistant professor must then apply for on an open-competition basis.

with him or her. It can make me incredibly angry, so it's a bit of a cop-out [that I don't do anything about it].

The assistant professor hides his anger. He avoids confronting his colleague on the grounds that it 'might backfire' on him later. He tries to modify his impulse to anger by rationalising the situation, but without great success. This is indicated by his description of his own behaviour as constituting 'a bit of a cop-out'. In a second example, the interviewer asks another assistant professor whether his friendliness towards certain (powerful) individuals is based on strategic considerations. He answers:

> I'd like to be able to say a categorical, "No" to that, but there's no doubt that ... I mean, I've never felt that someone actually went over the limit with me. But there's no doubt that you're slower to indicate where the limits are when people are higher up in the hierarchy. I wouldn't say that I go around being friendly just to get into people's good books. It's a bit more the other way round. There are some things you don't protest about, even though deep down you know very well that you would never have put up with that kind of thing from someone who didn't have some kind of power over you, you know what I mean? You really feel that a lot as a PhD fellow, and as a research assistant and as an assistant professor too. They are the [powerful] people, who will be deciding at some point whether or not you are qualified to go up the next rung on the ladder. I suppose this will continue – it's also the professors who decide whether or not you are professor material, if that's the way you want to go. Still, I hope I don't go around scratching too many backs (laughs). But honestly, I feel quite certain that you do let yourself get pushed around – a lot more than you'd accept if people didn't have power over you.

Both excerpts illustrate the need to tame emotions, given the power structure at issue, but they also indicate some moral limits to this process. Expressions such as 'cop-out' and 'scratching too many backs' can be interpreted as indicators of an unacknowledged feeling of shame involved in the process of taming one's emotions.[3]

The politics of friendliness can be exercised by controlling negative emotions, but also by being strategically friendly and expressing positive feelings towards particular people, as this man, an associate professor, sought to make clear:

> There's no doubt that sometimes you feel that people are expressing friendly attitudes towards views that you have good reason to think they weren't quite so friendly towards earlier. It could be a strategic choice or else it's just a matter of liking or disliking certain people. I'm not sure whether people use feelings

---

3 According to Scheff, the use of self-deprecating words may be verbal markers of unacknowledged shame. Scheff's theory is presented in Chapter 8.

strategically. I haven't thought about that. But with regard to friendliness, sometimes you can't understand why some guys are being friendly towards some group or other, and then it turns out that the simple reason has to do with some kind of strategic battle of interests.

The politics of friendliness guarantees that criticism will be withheld. Talk is silver, but silence can be gold. Thus, according to one woman, an assistant professor:

> IP: You mustn't say too much, because then you reveal yourself too much. You reveal yourself when you show your feelings. What you say in the heat of the moment is often something you'll regret later. So you have to think twice about what you say – and one isn't always able to do that. I've probably said some things – happily forgotten now – that I'm sure I regretted later.
>
> I: What do you think would have happened if you had talked about it [feelings regarding colleagues' assessment of her work]?
>
> IP: I think it would have come straight back and hit me like a boomerang.

It can prove difficult to maintain the politics of friendliness. Assistant professors can be disappointed and lose confidence and belief in Academia as an organisation. For example, one assistant professor describes how angry he is about what he describes as 'disgraceful employee politics' in his department, 'lack of responsible leadership' and 'deceitful allocation of blame to others'. The consequence is:

> I don't feel any loyalty to the department either. They get what they've paid for. I'd like to get a permanent position. I'd also like to change a few things if I do get one. But if I do get one, I won't feel any obligation towards anything except the terms of my contract. If it suits my own plans better to go somewhere else in the world for a few years or move to a different institution, I don't mind exploiting the opportunities in the Danish system for that purpose so long as it benefits me. I don't feel any sense of responsibility towards the department.

For this assistant professor, friendliness has become a cliché and does not express any real sense of support or solidarity. Yet, he nevertheless tries to observe the norms of friendliness.

> You try to behave in a proper way to everyone. You say hello and you try to force a neutral hello out of them. But there are people whose sense of superiority makes it hard for them to get a "hello" out of their mouths – also in university departments. Eh-h (long pause), but you have to try to some extent to set a positive mood somehow.

Friendliness as a feeling rule is a representative feeling that is expressed as an open attitude and a neutral tone, in which feelings are not revealed. Friendliness, however, is also a necessary strategy, given the particular structure of Academia. It is especially important if one's position is insecure. Assistant professors need to maintain friendly relationships with everyone. For this reason, they pursue a politics of friendliness, refrain from criticising others, try to retain a neutral position in ongoing conflicts, and to remain on friendly terms with everyone. This strategy entails different ways of handling emotions, which in turn can evoke other feelings such as shame or guilt.

The Deceiving Game

The politics of friendliness is important, but there are also other rules about how to gain visibility in the world of Academia. We must present ourselves to our academic colleagues – who, structurally speaking, are our competitors – as being academically competent. This presentation of self takes place on an ongoing basis, in conversations between colleagues, at research seminars, in workshops, at conferences and in other settings in which the researcher and his or her results are assessed.

Research is a process directed at solving problems and tackling difficult challenges. Hope and confidence and belief in one's research project alternate with despondency, uncertainty and doubt. Combined with Academia's specific structure, the uncertainties inherent in doing research give rise to fear of critical remarks on the part of colleagues. One PhD fellow expressed the problem this way:

> Fear, that is the thing that's transparently clear – not just among the PhDs, but in the whole culture of research as such. People are dead scared of not being good enough. Because one way or another they don't have much else to offer except their brains, do they? That's all we have to offer in this culture, and if someone shoots you down and cuts your work to pieces in front everyone else, people get dead scared. Yes, they are afraid of that. That's the way I see it.

The fear of not making the grade permeates the entire research culture, but revealing doubt and uncertainty would be breaking the feeling rules of Academia. One assistant professor says:

> That feeling of, "Do you know what? I don't know whether this is good enough", is a no-go in this system. There's no way you'd get away with that – almost disregarding how good it is – because it's so fundamental to everything you do in here that you are good enough. There's a really tough exclusion process on the basis of your qualifications all the way up through the system. So, you can't start out saying, "I haven't a clue whether I'm good enough to do this." But you can start by saying, "I don't really have a handle on this paper yet. This is a new area

for me and I haven't really been able to think it through yet. So, any responses to that?" I'm sure there are other people sitting around the table and thinking [the same]. I've done that myself tons of times. I've been on the point of packing it all in. I've said to myself: "You can be a case worker in a municipality in Jutland or something like that. There probably wouldn't be anyone there who'd demand too much of you," – because the pressure of expectations [at university] is extreme. A lot of it is self-generated, of course, but it's there. There's no doubt about that. I'd be damned surprised if all of us thought we could live up to that all of the time. I don't think we can, but that is not something one says in a more public, academic forum.

Academia is an elitist organisation engaged in research at the highest level. The selected few are therefore expected to display perspicacity, control and authority at all times. But this is a facade, as pointed out by one woman, an assistant professor:

I can see that people, who are 20 years older than me, are still just as nervous. They're just as worried about not being good enough, and have just as many problems with deadlines and stuff like that. I think that's pretty dreadful because I know how bright they are, how qualified they are and how competent. Yet, they still have that problem. You're inclined to hope that it's only at the beginning that it's so hard, and that it'll be much easier later on. But that's not the way it is apparently.

If everyone has feelings of this kind, why are they kept hidden? One assistant professor says:

Unfortunately, I think what governs the way we behave toward each other has to do with not wanting to expose too much of ourselves. So that is why nobody would want to do that voluntarily.

Another assistant professor says:

IP: It is OK to talk about limited fiascos.

I: What does that mean?

IP: That means for instance that if one has spent a month trying to run something or other down to the ground [in the library], and what one thought was to be found simply was not there at all. One has wasted that time and is about to go around the bend. I can talk about that kind of thing. "Do you know what?" "Now I've bloody well done it again." "That's not good at all." "What on earth will I do?" But real doubt about my own worth – which always turns up at some point in a fruitful research process – I wouldn't dream of revealing that. They might just believe it.

We can talk about 'limited fiascos' that we have under full academic control. But if we reveal the existential doubt that also belongs to the research process, we risk being classified as incompetent researchers, unfit for the task at hand.

Academia requires an academic facade. 'In Academia, you very quickly become a public academic person', noted one assistant professor. This applies in formal settings, but just as much in informal settings such as during coffee breaks or in the lunchroom. The following excerpts show how small cracks in the academic facade are met with ridicule, or lead to being ignored. The interviewer asks about embarrassing experiences and an assistant professor responds:

> I mean, if you've read an article and then in a discussion manage to blurt out something that makes no scientific sense whatsoever – that shows that you're not thinking straight. Or if we're chatting in a group of three or four and you say: "Well, the way I see it is such and such" and then people say, "What on earth do you mean by that? That sounds completely cracked," then you feel really embarrassed. You sit in the office afterwards feeling really terrible and just cursing yourself for saying something so stupid. We can also be in a banal situation like a coffee break when I say that an organism has such and such genes, and they are important for something or other. Then I'm told that I'm completely wrong and that what I have just said was utter bullshit. Then I just clam up, because I can see that what I said was rubbish. That's really embarrassing, just so incredibly embarrassing.

Public academic mistakes are punished. As another assistant professor says:

> The tone can be really harsh. "Just a moment, what you're saying is utter nonsense." The reaction is harsh – you're just ignored for the rest of the discussion. That's so hard to take, you know? Saying, "That's utter nonsense," and then they just carry on the discussion. The worst thing is that they are so dismissive. That's a situation I know very well.

The worst thing about academic mistakes is the risk of being labelled as stupid.

> You're always scared of being seen as stupid, but I don't feel …, I mean, there and then I think, oh God, they must think I'm a real idiot, but then as the day goes on one doesn't care so much about it.

The assistant professor survives, but being deemed 'stupid' is one of the most stigmatising categories in Academia (Hasse 2003).

Everyone encounters doubt and uncertainty, however. The culturally legitimate way to handle these feelings is to hide them behind an academic facade of control, certainty and perspicacity. I term this strategic handling of emotions 'the deceiving game' because everyone plays this game and everyone knows that everyone plays it. The deceiving game presupposes that emotion work is undertaken. On this point, the interviewees described physical techniques such as the use of tranquillisers or breathing exercises, cognitive techniques designed to distinguish research from the person of the researcher,[4] as well as the use of techniques designed to bolster a facade, such as the use of obscure jargon, prestigious references and name dropping.[5] The assistant professors and PhD fellows also describe emotion work undertaken collectively, such as trial presentations of papers as a rehearsal.

Some are better at keeping up the required facade than others, however, as one assistant professor expresses it:

> Some people have an incredibly good way of getting out of difficulties – by changing the subject, for example. I mean, if you're talking about an article, and the person you're talking to isn't quite up to speed with it, he can change the subject: "By the way, have you read this article?" about something or other. Suddenly, you're in a whole new discussion, and you can quickly end up that way, you know. But I don't do that, so situations like that get me down a bit.

The organisational conditions for the deceiving game are the specific structure of Academia and the way in which research tends to fuel the production of uncertainty and doubt. When we play the deceiving game, we hide our uncertainty and fear behind the facade of perspicacity, control and authority, thereby expressing the representative feelings of Academia. The deceiving game can function as a protective measure, a strategic presentation of the self, and in some cases can develop into bluff in the sense that one pretends for strategic reasons to have knowledge and competence that one does not in fact have.[6] In my analysis, the deceiving game emerges first and foremost as a protective measure that serves to confirm the feeling rules of Academia by demonstrating control and authority, as well as the proscriptions against revealing uncertainty, fear and doubt.

The deceiving game unfolds on many levels: in ongoing everyday interaction, in seminars, workshops and conferences when research results are presented for colleagues to scrutinise, and in mental preparation for these confrontations. Various aspects of the deceiving game were most clearly highlighted in interviews with PhD fellows and assistant professors. They were in the process of learning

---

    4   The cognitive distinction between the project and the person, according to Ehn and Löfgren (2004: 44), is a norm at PhD seminars, where PhD fellows must learn to accept criticism without taking it personally.

    5   Hochschild (2003) draws a distinction between 'deep-acting', as techniques designed to transform an actual emotion, and 'surface-acting', designed to transform a person's surface presentation of self. The techniques described correspond to Hochschild's distinction.

    6   See Wagner (1977) for an analysis of bluff in Academia.

this game, and were inclined to view it as being a culturally legitimate and wise strategy to follow. Some of them, however, also saw it as being a problematic way to handle one's feelings. Some, but not all, were successful at playing this game.

Ventriloquism[7]

Recognition by one's colleagues is the reward of scientific research, and recognition gives rise to pride. Pride and the cultural regulation of pride are the next topics to be considered.[8]

The interviewees describe pride in the context of academic successes such as having articles accepted by high-ranking journals, getting books published by recognised publishers, obtaining positive reviews, research grants and academic appointments. Generally, however, it is perceived as 'unacademic' or boastful to display pride in or delight about such accomplishments. This finding corroborates the results of the survey among assistant professors (Bloch and Dalsgård 2002), which identified a number of prohibitions that can be interpreted as aspects of a more general prohibition against the display of pride: boasting, using one's elbows, openly seeking power and feeling that one is better than other people.

The following examples illustrate how assistant professors handle this tension between pride and the prohibition against displaying pride. A recently appointed associate professor describes a situation in which he felt satisfaction and pride.

> IP: When I got the associate professorship, I was really pleased, especially because the position was advertised and the competition was tough. Yes, I felt really proud of getting that.
>
> I: How did you express that feeling?
>
> IP: I didn't, but I was happy that others did it for me (chuckles). You can't go around showing off at the university, but I was fine with that.
>
> I: Do you think your colleagues could tell that you were pleased and proud or ...?
>
> IP: No, I really don't think so. No, definitely not, it was like, it was ... no, not really. I tried to hide it.
>
> I: You tried to hide it?

---

7   This metaphor has been borrowed from one of the interviewees.

8   In cultural terms, pride is an ambiguous emotion that can refer to arrogance and vanity or to self-esteem and joy. The interviews were designed to elucidate pride in the latter sense, but this did not of course exclude that episodes referring to other aspects were also described.

> IP: Yes, among other things, by just carrying on working and not really celebrating it in any way. It's to do with the tradition in the department. We don't have much in the way of delighted reactions in this department – not even for an article in a good journal. When a good article is accepted, you say, "Good" and then you just carry on.

The interviewer continues:

> I: But if you have had an article accepted, is that something you would go and tell your colleagues about?
>
> IP: No, one just doesn't do that, and that's because there's always some competition going on between the different people in a department – and that means that one doesn't want to embarrass anyone. One doesn't want to … one doesn't want to … (laughs a little). It sounds strange, but one doesn't want to seem boastful – like if one comes out saying, "I've just had an article accepted for [well-known journal]." One keeps quiet about things like that. Maybe some people might find it easier to talk about. But the general feeling is that you don't boast about stuff like that. One just doesn't do that.

This associate professor identifies competitive relationships as the reason for his silence. This implies that his success is actually a threat to others. He does not want to embarrass others in the event that they do not share his delight. Recognition is the reward of Academia, such that the prohibition against displaying pride is shrouded in ambivalence. This is expressed in the associate professor's remark that some people are better than others at drawing the spotlight to their successes. The interviewer asks what he himself thinks about someone who talks about his or her own successes. He replies:

> IP: To be quite honest, you feel good if it's one of your closest friends or a good colleague that you think deserves it. But if it's someone that doesn't deserve it, you feel pretty bad about it. I think those are normal human reactions.
>
> I: When you say, "Doesn't deserve it" what do you mean? What does it take for a person not to deserve it?
>
> IP: Sometimes you might just get lucky with an experiment, or be fortunate enough to be involved in a colleague's work. I'm sure it's a feeling everyone in the department has. You know, feeling annoyed that others are doing TOO well (laughs a little) – if it's undeserved, you know?

The success achieved by others can lead to suspicion about the reasons for that success. Was it deserved, just a matter of luck or due to something else? The associate professor does not want to generalise, however. He says:

There's a lot of psychology in it because you tell some people, but not others, since you know what they're like. You know that that fellow will be annoyed about it, that one won't, and this one won't mind hearing about it. That's simply the way it is.

Despite competitive relationships, some don't mind hearing about the success of others, while some do mind. The interviewer asks an assistant professor whether she tells others about her academic successes. She confirms that she does and says of her colleagues' reaction:

Yes, but, umm, [they react] positively, I think. But there aren't so many people I would tell. I'm on the editorial board of a journal, And with the colleagues there one speaks a bit more freely in some way or other, because you're not direct competitors. Umm, so, no, I don't talk about stuff like that with so many in my own department. My older colleagues don't see me as a competitor in that way. I suppose they're happy when things go well for me. But with my own immediate colleagues – the assistant professors – that's where the problem is.

The closer one gets to one's direct competitors, the more one keeps quiet about one's joys and successes. This entails, as one man, an assistant professor, puts it:

In this department, people don't find out that you've produced an article until the reference appears in the yearbook. Before then, people quite simply don't know anything about it.

One has to be careful about displaying joy and pride in the successes of one's research, and this also applies to successes in one's teaching duties. One woman, an assistant professor, describes the norms regarding the expression of pride and satisfaction with one's teaching. She describes how she is pleased about and proud of her students' positive evaluation of her teaching. The interviewer asks whether she had revealed her pride and satisfaction, and she answers:

IP: No, only to the extent that ... I talked about it, of course (laughs), but I only did that at home. So that... No, it's quite private.

I: So nobody in the department heard you say: "Yes! I did it"?

IP: No, there wasn't, there wasn't.

I: Do you have to restrain your pride and satisfaction? Is there any reason that you have not posted it on your office door, for example, or told all your colleagues?

> IP: No, I don't think so. It's just a question of ordinary politeness and ordinary modesty. You don't do that, of course you just don't do that. If there are colleagues who ask how things are going I might say, "Yes, things are fine. I got a really nice evaluation, and I'm pleased about that." So in that kind of way you might say something, but you wouldn't just blurt it out without being asked.

Teaching has the character of a private room. Telling others about successful teaching is a breach of academic etiquette. However, not everyone is equally modest about their successes. As one man, an assistant professor says, some are better than others at expressing pride in their own performance, because they can present their successes in a legitimate way.

Below, a woman describes the conditions for showing pride in a legitimate way. This assistant professor says: 'I've just boasted about her [a bright PhD student) here at lunch'. However, this 'boasting' does not happen:

> ...out of the blue. The situation was that this colleague was engaged in something along the same lines [as the bright PhD student]. So, I offered to contact this student on the grounds that what she does is bloody good. And this went down very well: "I'd really like to see that."

The assistant professor then defines the conditions for talking about a success, as follows:

> Point 1: there must be something to be proud of, but umm (pause), point 2, it must either just have happened, so you come running out saying, "You won't believe what just happened," or it must be something that other people will find useful. Apart from those, it also helps if you can tell it as a funny story, so then you can get away with sneaking in the fact that you've done well, you know?

There must be something to be proud of since, as the assistant professor says:

> Colleagues that are blatant boasters, and always saying what they did and why, are really embarrassing. I'm talking about men here, since they're mostly the ones that do that. People are so sick of them. They don't want to listen to them. These men have done it all. They've written books, and they've done this and they've done that. Of course they have. It's expected of them. So, it's more about making it into a funny story, then you can get away with letting people know that you think you've done well, you know?

In addition 'it must be something that other people will find useful', such as an academic tip or a funny anecdote in which, as the assistant professor says, 'You can get away with letting people know that you think you've done well.' This assistant professor is very aware of which types of success should be actively highlighted for one's colleagues in one of these ways, and which types should not. She says:

> I'm very careful about saying when I've done something outside the department. I mean, I and many [academics] live in an [academic] world. That means that you don't have to announce everything. I never say when I've had an article in a journal, or held something for my own professional colleagues. They know about those, of course. They are the ones that should say something [about those events], so there it's actually the other way around. But I also work a lot with [another academic group], hold courses for them, and have given a presentation at their annual conference, and so on. They [her colleagues] don't have a chance of knowing about those things if I don't tell them. So, I do get around to letting them know in one way or the other. Mostly in the form of – well, that's a characteristic of this department, that it's a place where you tell things in the form of anecdotes. One describes a funny episode that happened at this of that conference, from which it emerges that I was present, that I was one of the keynote speakers.

These principles are further explained by another assistant professor. He is just finishing up a major project that he is really proud of and pleased with. He says:

> I've worked on this subject for a long time, now I've finished it, I've added the last comma, and isn't that just great. Now those [joy and delight] are legitimate feelings. But the story about all the awful things you had to go through to get this far, that is a low form of self-promotion that can be rather tiring in the long run. I'm sure you know the situation from dinner parties, [people that talk about themselves all the time].

He continues:

> The ordinary work of building up a project is just a question of doing your job. That's not so interesting. But if you sit down and describe how a particular piece of information has now finally fallen into place, there's a lot of interest in that – you know, the little hurrah-anecdotes about how I finally sorted it out. That feeling of getting something to fall into place is really something you phone home about, or you open your door and say, "Something really fantastic just happened here!"

The success must have a novelty dimension, or be something that has just happened. Yet the assistant professor does not open his door to announce his delight. Instead, he tells of his success in the form of a 'ray of sunshine' story.

> No, OK, I told it as a little ray of sunshine story to my closest colleagues – well, not actually my closest colleagues, since there's a difference between the people you work closely with academically and the people you have lunch with. The people I have lunch with are in all kinds of other fields, and they are the ones that usually hear my little ray of sunshine stories. They were right on the beam with

this one. They think it's good fun. So they nod in agreement and think that this guy has probably hit the nail on the head. But it has to do with choosing one's story, doesn't it? It's a matter of telling a story which is unusual and funny along the lines of, "A funny thing happened on the way to the baker's." It's an anecdote of that type, and nothing else. It's not a big, pompous presentation about having achieved a breakthrough. It's the kind of story you tell, tongue in cheek, with the idea that it's going to be received well because it's my baby that's waving to you and I want you to wave back.

There is a code for the legitimate expression of pride and joy:

It belongs to the code that one puts oneself in the background and then foregrounds something else – your material – that you use, so to speak, the same way as a ventriloquist, This gives one the opportunity to say, "Isn't it interesting?" But at the same time one gets the opportunity to present oneself as the person who has got the insight and now is presenting things in an order that makes the whole thing seem new and fantastically interesting.

This is a complicated code that is learned:

By imitation, just like one learns tacit codes of behaviour anywhere. I mean, a one-sided, jubilant presentation of one's own achievements is not going to go down well – that is, if one puts oneself at the centre of the story. It is permissible, I would say, within the little anecdote, because it's presented as an amusing little story. But it is not appropriate to put oneself at the centre of the story.

Pride is shrouded by ambivalence. Most interviewees describe the experience of feeling proud of successes and achievements, but some decline to acknowledge this feeling. One man, an assistant professor, says:

There's nothing wrong with my self-esteem, but I wouldn't call it pride. I believe that I do my work well, and I also believe that I fulfil both my teaching and research obligations at a level that meets reasonable demands – in some respects a bit more than that. But pride is not the word for it.

Even though the assistant professor will not acknowledge the feeling of pride, he does admit that for strategic reasons he allows a few words to fall in the right places about his successes:

I can mention it [success], upwards in the system, but that's just to a teaching supervisor. When you're an assistant professor, you sometimes have to make sure that things get mentioned. I mean, there's no reason to hide your light under a bushel all of the time (chuckles).

According to Pierre Bourdieu, recognition is the reward system of Academia. Everyone is proud of their successes, but they are also aware of the prohibition against expressing these feelings. It is culturally legitimate to circumvent this prohibition by means of ventriloquism, by wrapping one's pride in an entertaining or amusing anecdote. But why this ambivalence about displaying pride more openly when recognition by colleagues is the reward of the academic?

The philosopher of science, Hagstrom (1972), has an explanation for this. His theory takes its point of departure in the view that research is not a commodity for sale, but rather a form of gift-giving. Researchers offer their results to the scientific community and acceptance of the gift, according to the logic of gift-giving, entails the recognition of the status of the giver. In the world of science, acceptance thus entails recognition of the giver as a valued researcher. The logic of gift-giving, however, also entails the principle that gifts are offered without the expectation or calculation of a gift in return. Accordingly, researchers will deny that they undertake research in order to gain recognition. The researcher undertakes research for the sake of research. Nevertheless, recognition has *de facto* significance for the researcher. This significance is made apparent by, among other things, the reactions – sometimes, the open hostilities – triggered by the foiling of expected recognition. The logic of gift-giving captures the paradox that although science is a value in itself, recognition is nevertheless desired by the scientist. According to Hagstrom's theory, the prohibition against coveting recognition has its roots in the long established academic conception that research is undertaken for its own sake. This entails that the prohibition against the display of pride is a representative feeling prohibition that is firmly embedded in the values of research.

The researcher longs for recognition, however, which is why ventriloquism serves as a legitimate means of handling one's pride. Ventriloquism is legitimate insofar as it accords with the logic of gift-giving. It is a feature of ventriloquism that someone offers a tip, some valuable information or an entertaining story, which the recipients acknowledge, offering in return their acceptance of the underlying message that the speaker has achieved an academic success. In principle, when colleagues exchange gifts in the form of information and entertainment there can be no expectation of reciprocity, but an expectation of gratitude is implied, and thereby of receiving something in return.

Hagstrom understands the prohibition against pride as being grounded in the ideas and values associated with research as an activity. However, some of the interviewees in this study view this prohibition as being a tactful way of handling their competitive relationships. Given competition, the successes achieved by others can be perceived as threats making it hard to share their delight. Some interviewees interpreted and justified this prohibition on the basis of a principle of solidarity. One associate professor describes it this way:

> Well it could just as well be an expression of something cultural – that one tries to maintain some kind of culture of solidarity, in which no one is worth more than anyone else in some way or other. After all we are researchers. One could

say that the basic idea of such a research institution – or behind such a research institution – is, after all, that it is difficult to compare research [in different fields]; it is difficult to measure research. That's why I think that it is embedded in our culture, and there is probably something healthy in that – then no one in that way ... [is better than others].

This man views the prohibition against pride as a cultural means of protecting oneself from mutual competition by means of a form of solidarity in which no one is worth more than anyone else. Tact of this kind also implies that the individual's successes, and thereby pride, to the extent they are expressed at all, are usually expressed to people who are not direct competitors.

The Social Order of Visibility

The politics of friendliness, the deceiving game and ventriloquism are strategic ways of handling emotions in order to present or position oneself as a pleasant and academically competent actor within the framework of the given culture of emotions. A number of studies show that academic settings, which are seemingly devoted to academic discussion, actually concern ways in which the actors seek to gain position (Gerholm and Gerholm 1992, Henriksson et al. 2000, Ehn and Löfgren 2004). Assistant professors, associate professors and full professors seem to have a tacit agreement that the politics of friendliness, the deceiving game and ventriloquism are the legitimate and strategically appropriate ways of handling emotions. The deceiving game and ventriloquism are not available to everyone, however, for as an assistant professor points out:

> To be proud and happy you must have fought your way to a position in which other people could be bothered hearing that you are proud and happy. For example, we have some temporary staff that come and go. Because they are temporary, it is very difficult for them to achieve a position in which they might allow themselves to show pride and delight, unless they have, well, exceptional personal charisma, which some of them may have. But there are lots of other temporary staff that nobody ever listens to, no matter what they might have to say.

Social position thus also determines access to strategic emotion management.

Summary

In formal terms, academic life is about producing knowledge at the highest scientific level. In real terms, this life is just as much about ensuring one's visibility in an academically proper fashion. I have highlighted some of the emotions that arise from the structure and culture of Academia, and have identified a number of culturally recognised ways of handling these emotions. By means of the politics of friendliness, the deceiving game and ventriloquism, emotions are diverted, suppressed or transformed, while at the same time these strategies express academically representative feelings. The politics of friendliness, the deceiving game and ventriloquism each constitute aspects of the tacit, but culturally recognised, culture of emotions in Academia. They are present as unspoken, but common knowledge among the academic population. I have called them strategies because everyone, whether they have mastered the strategies or not, presents them as culturally acknowledged ways of presenting oneself and gaining visibility in acceptable ways. My analysis has drawn primarily on excerpts from the assistant professors' narratives. The politics of friendliness, the deceiving game and ventriloquism were by no means restricted to this group, but perhaps due to their position in the academic hierarchy, assistant professors more readily presented examples of these strategies in detail. It is not enough to be aware of specific management strategies, however. As already indicated, access to these management strategies is conditioned by one's social position. But access is also conditioned by gender. Chapter 9 presents an analysis of the interplay between emotion management, social standing and gender.

Chapter 5
The Janus Face of the Peer Review

The peer review is the lifeblood of research in Academia (cf. Bourdieu 1975). This is the social structure that subjects research to the critical assessment of other researchers. The process of collective control and approval, which is a distinguishing characteristic of scientific research, is exercised by means of a variety of assessment committees that pronounce their judgement prior to publishing work in scientific journals, granting academic degrees, allocating funding for research projects and appointing tenured positions. Peer review also underlies ongoing academic discussion in the lunchroom, at research seminars and at conferences, during which competing colleagues pass judgement on each other's work.

The purpose of peer review is to ensure the production of research of the highest calibre, but the peer review is also a complex social structure that is based upon the structure of competitive relationships. The German sociologist, Georg Simmel (1970: 86–9), has described some of the feelings and attitudes that arise from competitive relationships. Competition differs from other types of struggle in that it does not necessarily entail direct confrontation between the parties, whose attention is instead concentrated upon a shared external goal or object. This also entails that 'moral instincts' are more easily submerged than is the case in direct confrontation, when any damage resulting from the struggle will be immediately apparent. By concentrating upon the object, rather than the competitor, competition can acquire the characteristic of cruelty, which is inherent in all forms of objectification. The cruelty at issue is not due to a desire to see others suffer, but rather to the absence of subjective considerations, such that the person of the competitor is placed in the background. When competition is the decisive factor in a given situation, our moral instincts regarding the ruthlessness of competition are offset by a satisfying sense that justice is being done, which can also be extended to include the vanquished party. Competitive relationships thus tend to promote both an objectification of the other and a moral sense of justice regarding the vanquished party. Simmel describes relationships in which there is consensus between competing parties regarding the rules of the game. This is not always the case in Academia, where a struggle between different scientific paradigms may render the conditions of competition less than clear cut. In addition, the formalised peer review is more complicated than simpler forms of competitive relationship, since power is asymmetrically distributed between the assessors and the assessed. It grants the assessor the power to approve or disapprove of the work accomplished by the person assessed.

The raison d'être of the peer review is collegial assessment of each other's scientific work, undertaken on the basis of objective scientific criteria. This can take place in a transparent, amicable, constructive and productive way. The structure of the peer review, however, also allows an objectification of the assessed person to take place, just as the asymmetric distribution of power in this relationship may tempt assessors to favour their own academic interests and ambitions.[1] The peer review thus has a Janus face. The dark side is illustrated here using the metaphor of the 'academic rapier'. This is followed by focusing on one of the key emotions of the peer review: the anger felt by both the assessor and the assessed. This chapter is based primarily on the narratives of associate and full professors.[2]

The Academic Rapier

Research is the object of critical discussion and assessment at seminars and conferences. Obscure passages become highlighted, reasoned argument is presented and omissions are pointed out. Critical discussion can degenerate into what Ehn and Löfgren (2004: 104) refer to as the 'disputation syndrome', or argument for the sake of argument, narrowly focused upon fault-finding and self-promotion. The interviewees in this study do not use this term, but some do speak about the 'academic rapier'. One PhD fellow puts it this way:

> Here, there is a kind of knightly tradition, like in fencing, when people keep throwing down the glove as a challenge and fighting each other off the court by using more sophistry than the others. I've thought about this a lot. I mean, the way people challenge each other in here is about challenging academic honour – taking the other person's honour, you know? It's like striking the rapier out of the hand of the other person.

---

1 Several scholars have questioned the objectivity of the peer review (Becher and Trowler 2001, Ehn and Löfgren 2004). Cole's studies of the validity of peer review with regard to the identification of scholars, who later become productive researchers, can also be mentioned. Cole found that rejected applicants later proved to be more productive researchers than applicants who had been assessed positively (Cole 1983).

2 In Denmark, associate and full professors have permanent tenure. The difference between an associate and a full professor lies in salary and prestige, while they spend the same ratio of their time on research (40 per cent) and have the same commitments (teaching, supervision, assessment, administrative functions, etc.). During the 1970s and 1980s, Danish universities pursued a policy which entailed that relatively few vacant professorships or new professorships were filled. This period was called the era of associate professors. The number of professorships increased significantly during the 1990s, primarily in the form of fixed-term 5-year appointments.

The academic rapier is used to make hits and to strike the weapon from the other person's hand. The tone of this struggle can be very raw. A foreign associate professor describes his Danish colleagues in the following way:

> They are more war-like, and there is an aggressive and often ironic attitude. Before I started here my predecessor told me I shouldn't get upset if some people became a bit vicious, because many of them have that kind of facade.

This struggle can escalate into a public 'assassination', as told by one associate professor:

> It has happened a few times at our annual meeting, which is usually quite enjoyable. Some colleagues have had their data material under scrutiny, which ended up with the view – announced at a big gathering like that – that this was the greatest load of shit they had ever produced. You just sat there thinking: this is really pretty embarrassing. I think everyone there felt that things had in some way or another gone right over the limit. After all, anything can be torn to shreds. One can always apply those ten criteria for an article and then pull it apart bit by bit. But I think that some of that kind of criticism is pointless in some way or other. It was more to show off that the other person [the critic] had something to say, than to contribute something. It was not constructive, and it doesn't advance anything. It was just a matter of bringing the man down or else just promoting one's own position.

Apart from an academic assessment based on objective scholarly criteria, this associate professor indicates that there are other motives at play: bringing the other person down in order to gain the upper hand. The peer review makes this possible because, as the associate professor says, one can always pull apart a piece of research. One can always find something to criticise. There are normative limits to destructive criticism, but just where these limits lie often remains unclear.

The peer review in these examples is conducted in a public setting. The traditional peer review in the more narrow sense takes place behind closed doors in assessment committees, appointment committees or through the medium of anonymous referees. The academic community selects expert researchers and authorises them to undertake assessments and to include or exclude applicants.

Attention will now be turned to the emotions of these assessors and to what I term 'assessor anger'.[3]

---

3 Four emotion groups, including anger, were investigated in the present study. Anger, it transpired, was most often related to peer review in the narratives of interviewees. However, this study was not designed to explore feelings related to the peer review as such. While anger is related to peer review, it should be emphasised that peer review yields a basis for many other feelings such as pride and delight.

Assessor Anger

Several interviewees describe a feeling of anger while undertaking their work of assessment. This was rather surprising. Assessment involves judgment of the work of others on the basis of objective criteria, and anger can hardly be conceived as a legitimate emotion in this context. This anger is described on the part of individual assessors, but also as a collective feeling shared by the members of assessment committees. The following examples illustrate the ways in which anger is described, first in conjunction with the assessment of a PhD thesis:

> I get angry when someone wants the glory of academic credit, but doesn't respect what that demands. If someone is careless about methodological criteria, careless about giving credit to colleagues, when credit is due, then I get angry. And I get that out of my system during my opposition.

And regarding the assessment of master's theses:

> I get angry about this, and I put that anger into my first comment. I crack the whip and I give them a real telling off. Then in the second round I calm down – I've given vent to all my irritation and anger. I'm more balanced then, because I can very well see that I've been in too much of a rage (laughs a little), and then it end up with… Well, a piece of work I've raged and ranted about might easily end up with a B grade.

As one example of collective anger:

> I think as a matter of fact it often happens in assessment committees. There are others besides me that need to get all that, ah, all that anger out in the open, before we get to the point of saying: "OK, now what are we going to commit to paper about this?" Then we restrain ourselves, and it's easier for us to restrain ourselves when we've been able to put all our irritation and anger into words for each other. I've experienced this several times, both in doctoral assessments and appointment committees. I think it gives a sense of trust – a trusting relationship that doesn't have anything to do with personal acquaintance with each other. It has to do with our acquaintance with each other as academics, as colleagues. When we've talked about our irritation, we know where the others stand. It establishes a mutual trust, which in turn allows for a greater degree of openness.

But what does this anger described by assessors concern and what is its cause? A single answer to these questions is hardly to be expected. One assessor accounts for angry feelings by referring to a sense of academic justice: 'Who dares to present a doctoral thesis that doesn't show respect for academic values?' This anger is a legitimate moral feeling that motivates the assessor to document that the candidate at issue is not deserving of academic merit. Yet some of these excerpts indicate that anger is virtually lying in wait – as a point of departure for assessment. Such anger may play a role in a type of mobilisation process leading to academic assessment, but it can also be interpreted as a form of anger that arises from the relationship between the assessor and the assessed. Applicants, after all, seek to gain academic merit, challenging thereby an existing balance of power. This challenge, as such, can evoke irritation, anger and hostility on the part of assessors.[4] In that event, collective anger can be interpreted as a shared response to the same experience, and it can also be seen as a means of consolidating a sense of academic fellowship on the basis of a shared emotion. Collective anger, as pointed out by one of the assessors, can yield a relationship of trust between assessors. By expressing their anger, they can show where they stand as academics and lay the foundations for a relationship of mutual trust, which can lead to a more nuanced view of the applicants' work. However, maintaining a sense of group solidarity can also become a goal in itself, one that is turned against the applicant in the form of undiplomatic statements. As one professor says:

> For my own part, I might say that one could perhaps have handled the situation a little more diplomatically. It is possible that... But the other members of the assessment committee weren't diplomats either! (laughs) Yes, we certainly didn't mince our words [in our assessment of a colleague]. The others were not exactly diplomatic either (small laugh).

Expressions such as 'not diplomatic' and 'didn't mince our words', accompanied by occasional laughter, paint a picture of an assessment committee that perhaps has been more concerned with confirming group solidarity among its members than with preparing an informative and respectful assessment of the applicants' work.

Assessments should be made according to objective criteria on an emotionally neutral basis. Nevertheless, it can be difficult to draw the line between objective assessment of academic merit and personal involvement on the part of the assessor. Here is an example of an attempt to resolve this conflict by appealing to an academic sense of justice. An assessor describes his thoughts and feelings about assessing a PhD thesis which, according to him, had attempted to refute his own research:

> You [the interviewer] mentioned shame and guilt, and on that front I had some really serious concerns about just how harsh I could allow myself to be in my assessment, even though there was very good reason to be harsh – since some of the work that was criticised [in this thesis] was my own academic work. That really put me on the spot, but I was ANGRY. And I was harsh and very sharp in my opposition. It had really given me a lot to think about. But I decided to,

---

4 Perceived shifts in the relative distribution of power, which are experienced as being caused by the other person, generate anger (cf. Kemper 1978a).

ah, to stick my neck out, as one says, you know? I mean, I decided to ignore the fact that I could be accused of mixing my personal reactions into it. Because I simply ... (stammering:), ah, I could, I am convinced that it concerned academic criteria [that were being challenged], so I pulled myself together and I said what had to be said.

Personal motives are not a legitimate feature of assessments and in this case are explained away by referring to an academic sense of justice. Doubt, discomfort and shame still persist nevertheless, and later in the interview are expressed in the form of anger towards colleagues who had been critical of this assessment.

However, assessors also have other feelings apart from anger in connection with assessments. As one assessor says:

> I can certainly also be incredibly pleased about and grateful for a doctoral thesis or a master's thesis that one is given the opportunity to assess. Because it is especially when you have to assess the work that you really get to the bottom of it and you can be terribly pleased about that. It might be a review, a doctoral thesis, a master's thesis or some other examination work. I can get a lot of enjoyment out of that, and sometimes I can even feel decidedly grateful – because it, ah, touches upon something one is pleased to have described or unravelled.

Assessment work is by no means an emotionally neutral activity. Yet, feelings – not least that of assessor anger – are illegitimate, and are therefore not acknowledged features of the peer review. Assessor anger can be a morally legitimate emotion, but it can also be an anger that mobilises for opposition, a personally motivated feeling of anger, and it can be a group emotion that prepares the ground for negative or less respectful assessments under the guise of an academic sense of justice. As Ehn and Löfgren write: 'Academic experts do not usually wear silk gloves when assessing the contributions of others, and sometimes it seems as though they primarily wish to reveal academic shortcomings, rather than acknowledge the merits of applicants' (2004: 26–7). In principle, assessments are based on objective criteria, but personal and emotional criteria also play a significant role in assessments of the abilities of others. These aspects would seem to be at least as important as the more formal aspects of assessment.

The Anger of the Assessed

The peer review can bring paradigm battles, group rivalries and the feelings of assessors into play. This entails that the basis on which a given assessment has been made can be experienced as being far from clear. Assessments can be also perceived as being offensive, unfair or disrespectful. A majority of interviewees describe examples of assessments they had experienced as being offensive. These give rise to strong emotional reactions. This is how one interviewee describes an offensive peer review that had taken the form of a review of one of her academic works, undertaken by a colleague. She says:

> Yes, well, what can one say? Academic defeats can release those feelings [shame and guilt]. Apropos that, I can mention that I published a major piece of work a few years ago that gave rise to feelings of both pride and shame – because I thought myself that it was a good piece of work, even though there were some errors in it. On the whole, it got good reviews too. But there certainly were a few, I would say, that were nothing but expressions of what I would call academic envy, hate and small-mindedness. That kind of thing makes one depressed, but also ashamed that some people can behave in that way.

The interviewer asks whether she had confronted one of these offending colleagues, and she responds:

> I wouldn't dream of it. It [that review] was so nasty, on such a low level and so plain bad, that I would never take it up with him face-to-face – never!... Other people – who've experienced the same kind of treatment from him – have given him a piece of their mind, but I couldn't be bothered having anything to do with it.

The interviewee speaks of shame and of becoming depressed. She does not describe feelings of anger, but the words she uses when describing this review – 'nasty', 'low', 'bad' and 'small-minded' – can be interpreted as indications of a strong and sustained anger. However, this interviewee endeavours to transform her feelings towards her critic by categorising this person as being such a contemptible and despicable creature that she feels depressed and ashamed on his behalf. One might imagine that she would feel ashamed and depressed on her own behalf, but in her narrative these feelings are projected onto her critic. By interpreting her reviewer in this light, the interviewee seeks to neutralise the shame and anger that were presumably provoked by this review. The same pattern is illustrated by another interviewee in the following excerpt:

> Well, there is another of my colleagues who wrote a very offensive review of my [book] that made me really angry and cross. You can see it as a form of disrespect, also because there isn't really anything you can do about it. That's just the way things are... I complained to the editor and I also thought a good deal about writing to the person concerned. But the review was such a bad piece of work that it would be ridiculous to sit and write about it. It would just make the whole thing even more ridiculous, you know? I actually did make a few attempts at it last summer, until I found out that the only thing to do was just to let it wash away down the drain.

The review is described as being offensive and disrespectful, and the interviewee describes her own feelings about it in terms of anger. Her account shows that she does try to find a form of counter-attack, but she finally abandons this attempt, and thereafter tries to distance herself from the whole episode by characterising it as being quite ridiculous. She thus ends up using the same strategy as the first interviewee. She describes her critic and the review as being unworthy and ridiculous and in this manner seeks to neutralise her feelings of shame and anger.

The interviewees also describe episodes in which they had received positive assessments from a committee in the first round, but then later had been rejected or assessed as being unqualified by a subsequent committee.[5] One associate professor says:

> IP: It's actually a very competitive environment. If you are rejected, which I have actually been a few times, you are totally pissed off, disappointed, upset, angry and all the rest of it. I have applied [for a position] several times and been pronounced qualified, and then someone else was given the position. In one instance a few years ago, I thought the advertisement [for a position] completely matched me [my qualifications]. I was qualified for that. I just had to apply. So I did. There was a three-member committee, and they all pronounced me as qualified, and a majority recommended me [for the position]. But that was not allowed to happen, because the assessment committee was then expanded with a couple of extra members. Later I was told that in practice they had hardly had any meetings, you know? They were people who'd been told what to think, and then it was someone else they wanted to recommend.
>
> I: Intrigues?
>
> IP: Yeah, that's clear as a bell. But even so, it's still an unbearable state of affairs. So one might as well forget about it (little forced laugh).

This episode illustrates the fact that academic assessments are not so immutable that an assessment committee's recommendation cannot be reversed by the assessment of a subsequent committee. The process is one that evokes the experience of being rejected as a person, which in turn triggers feelings of disappointment, anger and

---

5 Situations of this kind can arise in the Danish system if it is decided to expand a 3-person appointment committee to a 5-person committee. All applicants must be assessed by such a committee and pronounced to be qualified or unqualified for the position at issue, whether unanimously or by a majority. Formerly, an appointment committee also nominated the person recommended for the appointment from among those deemed qualified. This system is referred to by many of the interviewees in the present study. In recent years, however, an appointment committee no longer recommends the successful applicant. This decision now rests with the Dean of the Faculty at issue, who selects the successful applicant from the list of applicants deemed qualified by the appointment committee. Higher authority, such as Head of Department or Dean of Faculty, is also usually involved in decisions to expand an appointment committee.

grief. It is 'unbearable', as the associate professor says, such that 'one might as well forget about it.' Yet, the question remains, whether it is possible to forget about feelings of this kind?

A common theme in these excerpts is that the assessed persons feel attacked, insulted and unfairly treated. They seek to forget or otherwise transform the many feelings that are triggered by these experiences by means of emotion work. Their narratives indicate that it is difficult for these persons to neutralise these feelings. But why are they not channelled into criticism of their assessors? The following excerpt from an associate professor's narrative indicates one reason why:

> Well, I've applied for a few [professorships]. I've also been pronounced "qualified", but I just didn't get the job. There's been a few times when I had to work on getting over it, you know – when I was really convinced that there was nepotism in the system. It's that Huey, Dewey and Louie thing – I've had that confirmed beyond doubt a couple of times. It is men on that level and men are assessing other men. I think it can make you very cross at times. You can also see it with the new professorships that are under consideration – they are planned with someone in mind, who just happens to fit in with some very rigorous norms. It's also a question of people knowing each other, and making room for each other, so they can all line up in a row together. Some of them have been following in each other's footsteps for years and they think they owe each other a few favours. That's the way it looks from the outside, but it's possible that it's just me being paranoid. But it was glaringly obvious for one of those positions. I'm convinced about that one, I have to admit. Several of us complained about that one, because the person who was recommended was not the best qualified on paper.

The interviewer asks what the result of the complaint was, and the associate professor answers:

> My experience of complaining upwards in the system – and now I've also participated in making some recommendations – is that complaints are a bloody waste of time. And I also have the impression that some people really feel that they get labelled in the wrong way if they complain. It's that fear again, of being noticed in the wrong way.

This associate professor speaks openly of nepotism, 'old boys' networks and partiality as being active elements of the peer review, but at the same time she moderates her statement by saying that she may be paranoid. This form of peer review takes place behind closed doors, and is a strong institution in Academia. It entails, according to this associate professor, that people who complain do not get anything out of it and also risk being labelled or looked down upon as being difficult. The associate professor therefore makes the reservation that she herself may be paranoid and, in the same way as several others, describes her feelings in terms of becoming 'cross'. That is to say, she and others characterise their feelings by using a somewhat derogatory term, which suggests that the speaker may be the difficult party. Viewed from this perspective, it is understandable that most opt to keep their feelings and criticism to themselves, since otherwise they will be sanctioned – as one of the associate professors laconically notes: 'that's just the way things are.'

Not everyone, however, is able to hide their anger about assessments, which they perceive as being offensive. The following excerpt concerns an assessor's description of a colleague's reaction to the news that the appointment committee had deemed him unqualified for a position for which he had applied. The first part of this excerpt was presented earlier in the introduction.

> He was angry, disappointed and upset by the assessment committee's recommendation, but he was also extremely incensed and quite beside himself – running around showing the recommendation to all his colleagues... In the end, he declared that he would not speak one more word to me ever again. Since then – and that was [some] years ago – he has looked right through me whenever we met, and we have never said hello to each other. What happened since is that he's been trying to sabotage some of the work I have been doing to get this department on the right tracks. This has given rise to a great many quarrels within the department and a major personal conflict. It has had some deeply felt consequences that have also affected personal relationships in here. It's also led to a couple of episodes in which people really let fly and let off a lot of steam, including myself. Any cooperation with that person will probably never again be possible.

This is a case in which explosive anger leads to involving an entire department in an assessment that was experienced as unfair. The injured party instigates open hostilities against members of the assessment committee, which spread through the entire department in question.

On the basis of these examples nothing can be concluded about the actual content or quality of the reviews and recommendations at issue. However, these examples do document that assessments can be experienced as offensive, as lacking respect for the applicant as a person or for that person's field of study, or merely as a manifestation of the assessors' personal or institutional interests. These experiences release strong emotions. Researchers identify with their research projects, such that an assessment of a researcher's work also functions as an assessment of that researcher as a person (Knorr Cetina 1982, Ehn and Löfgren 2004). Since the peer review is a strongly rooted institution in Academia, most academics seek to forget or by other means transform negative feelings of this kind. Seemingly, the authority of the peer review is contested at one's peril.

I have focused on the dark side of the Janus face. Most interviewees had both positive and negative experiences to relate with reference to the peer review. However, the selected excerpts are in no sense exceptional.

Distrust, Envy and *Schadenfreude*

Anger, shame and disappointment are emotions of the peer review, but a number of other emotions also arise from meritocratic competition at all levels within Academia. There is competition for scientific merit, but also for position within a number of ranking systems. Academia is obsessed with ranking systems, including the ranking of publishers, journals, citations, elected posts and honorary appointments, the source and size of research funds and the number of PhD scholarships (Becker and Trowler 2001, Ehn and Löfgren 2004, Schoug 2004, Bourdieu 1988). Yearbooks and departmental annual reports offer an excellent overview of current ranking systems. The constant vying for position, which is an on-going feature of academic life, gives rise to feelings of envy, schadenfreude and distrust. Here are some examples of these feelings and the ways they are handled. First are some examples of distrust. One woman, an associate professor, says:

> I've probably been a bit naïve about the competitive aspect of research. I feel that it is strange when colleagues set up a project that is very close to the work I'm doing myself, and then they don't talk about it openly and honestly – so that we could work together, instead of competing for the same things. I suddenly found out just recently that some people I work very closely with in other contexts had applied for funding from the same foundation that I had applied to – and our research projects had the same title and very similar content! I only got to hear about this because one of the people on the assessment committee let me know that they wouldn't be funding either of these two projects because they think we should cooperate. I feel myself that I was open and had told the people I work closely with about my project. They don't say openly that they are more or less doing a parallel study – now that surprises me.

Some researchers do not see each other as potential partners in a cooperative endeavour, but rather as rivals in a competition who are ready to take advantage of each other. Insofar as they distrust each other, their cards are kept close to the chest. An extreme manifestation of this distrust is expressed in fear of and suspicion about scientific theft or plagiarism. The interviewees in this study did not bring up these topics spontaneously. This may reflect the fact that they were largely drawn from rural research environments, in which researchers are engaged in investigating a range of different problems, such that issues regarding scientific theft tend to be less relevant.[6] Another reason may be that

---

6 According to Becker and Trowler (2001), scientific theft tends to occur more often in 'urban research environments', where researchers work in close competition on similar problems. The present study primarily regards 'rural research environments' (cf. Chapter 2), in which researchers work on a wide variety of different problems and would not benefit by stealing each other's work.

in rural environments the boundary between engaging in academic dialogue and stealing ideas is relatively hazy, such that an accusation of scientific theft may well rebound to the accuser with a further accusation that he or she is being paranoid or small-minded. As one associate professor says:

> I have experienced several times how people have been angry or disappointed [about colleagues taking their ideas and making them their own] – for example at academic seminars. They very consciously make a huge effort to act as if nothing is going on because it's not appropriate to say anything about that sort of thing. I've noticed that several times and I also think I ran into it once myself, when I said to myself, "Well now, that there, that is just a bit too close altogether to the line of argument I myself have made. There should be a footnote or something that actually… [inaudible sequence]." Or, even worse, they may get very close to some content or something [I have written]. Even then, you can't really start getting up on your high horse because the case is not so unequivocally clear that you can start yelling about scientific theft. Otherwise, I think one probably would do something about it.

The associate professor describes his suspicion of scientific theft. This accusation, however, is a serious matter, such that it rests with harbouring conflicting feelings of suspicion, distrust, disappointment, guilt and shame.

Envy is another feeling that arises from competitive relationships.[7] In his analysis of this emotion, Ben-Ze'ev (2000) distinguishes two types: 1) envy concerning a situation in which others have what we would like to have, which gives rise to a feeling of inferiority, and 2) envy about a situation in which others undeservedly have what we would like to have, which gives rise to a moral sense of injustice.

Envy entails social comparison and can therefore be evoked by all of the ranking systems in Academia. The following excerpt, drawn from a professor's narrative, exemplifies the first type of envy:

> There's that familiar feeling of jealousy and envy. It's here, there and everywhere. If a colleague suddenly has a book published by a prestigious publishing house you can get the feeling that you're lagging behind. That's the kind of dynamic you often see in here, because to a certain extent there's a competitive mentality. It's not so bad here as in [two other faculties], but it's there. Being the first and the best is what counts, just like in many other areas of life. If you feel others are overtaking you and leaving you behind, then of course the green-eyed monster shows itself in here too – just as it does everywhere else.

The professor describes the dynamic of envy in competitive relations. The success of one's colleague creates a social difference, a point of comparison that leaves

---

7   Envy is a key emotion in Academia. It is presented by Ehn and Löfgren (2004) as being virtually an occupational hazard of academic life.

one feeling overtaken and inferior, left behind in the company of the green-eyed monster. Envy is a despicable emotion, however, and therefore the professor seeks in several rounds to normalise his admission of the presence of envy by pointing out that it is present 'here, there and everywhere' and is even worse elsewhere – in other faculties. The interviewer asks whether the professor himself is familiar with the feeling of envy.

> IP: Yes, yes, I must admit I am. Of course I am.
>
> I: Do you try to hide that feeling or do you show it?
>
> IP: No, I wouldn't dream of showing it. I have to say, I keep it very well under wraps. Only my wife would be told anything about that.
>
> I: How do you keep it hidden?
>
> IP: Well, I pull down my mask and I offer my congratulations very nicely. Then one makes sure that one doesn't get into that situation too often by leading the field oneself (laughs). But then it's not always easy.

Envy is hidden behind the mask of friendliness. The professor then describes how he avoids being envious by making sure that he himself leads the field. This indication of superiority is then moderated by a small laugh and the admission that "it's not always easy". The following is an example of the second type of envy. Another professor says:

> Ah (pause), yes, it [envy] can certainly occur. Well yes, and perhaps in many different (pause) contexts. One is often dependent upon external funding for a project or for hiring a PhD fellow. Those funds are limited, so there's a lot of competition for them. One might sometimes feel somewhat envious if others get funding for a project that one doesn't consider to be nearly as good as one's own. But then again, it would be hard to say whether real envy was at issue there. That would depend on how one had ranked the competitor's project beforehand as compared to one's own. I mean, one can, of course, sometimes acknowledge that a project proposed by someone else is an excellent project that certainly deserves support, even though one has oneself also applied for funding from the same source. At other times one may have the view that some of these funding bodies are ranking these projects wrongly, and the colleague who obtained funding has a project that is vastly inferior to one's own. One might then feel a little envious about the fact that precisely that [the competitor's] project has paid off, you know? Perhaps that is a kind of envy.

In contrast to the previous interviewee, this professor is very cautious when speaking about envy. However, he does hesitantly admit to experiencing envy in the form of moral indignation when colleagues undeservedly obtain what he would like to have.

Malicious delight, or schadenfreude, is closely related to envy. Schadenfreude refers to gloating or gleeful feelings about the setback or misfortune that befalls another person. Like envy, schadenfreude arises from competitive relationships, but can be seen as the complement to envy. The former feeling is one of malicious delight in the failures of the other person, while the latter feeling is one of annoyance or fury about their success insofar as social comparison highlights one's own inferiority. Schadenfreude, alongside envy, is also a despicable emotion. This would seem to be the reason why interviewees only talked spontaneously about this feeling when describing the feelings of other persons. However, they were also asked how their colleagues reacted if they themselves were facing a setback in their academic careers. An associate professor, whose research had been subjected to offensive and unpleasant criticism according to his own account, answered this question in the following way:

> Yes, well there almost certainly were some that gloated about it, and then there were others who thought that that kind of carry on had been ridiculous and completely below the belt.

A professor answers as follows to a question about how his colleagues react to his academic fiascos:

> Well, they just say: "Oh! That is a shame," and then they take a bit of delight in it. I mean, that's just the way things are.

Distrust, envy and schadenfreude are feelings that are directly related to competitive relationships in Academia. Competition entails that one person's success is potentially the other person's fiasco, and vice versa. Distrust arises from competitive as compared with cooperative relationships in the struggle to gain resources and merit, while envy and schadenfreude are feelings that arise from social comparisons among colleagues, which can result in a sense of one's own inferiority, a sense of moral injustice or a sense of the other person's inferiority. These feelings are familiar features of everyday life in Academia, but are generally viewed as being despicable. As far as possible, therefore, they are hidden behind a friendly facade.

Summary

Peer review and meritocratic competitive relationships are social structures, the objective of which is to ensure the production of research of the highest calibre. These structures give rise to such feelings as anger, shame, distrust, envy and schadenfreude. The activity of doing research gives rise to feelings of passion, commitment and self-esteem, but also entails a particular vulnerability with regard to the recognition of its results by colleagues and equally strong feelings when such recognition is absent, contested or disputed.

Anger, shame, envy and schadenfreude are forbidden feelings in the emotional culture of Academia. They are therefore hidden behind a convivial and friendly facade. These feelings are recognised by many, and are defended by some as being inevitable features of a culture that nurtures excellence. Some of those who recognise these feelings distance themselves from them in a humorous fashion.

Chapter 6
The Politics of Laughter

Fear, anger and envy are among the feelings housed in Academia, but so are laughter, humour, irony and sarcasm. The interviewees were asked about episodes involving laughter. Laughter occurs in conjunction with humour, comedy, joy, delight and relief, but also in conjunction with mockery and gleeful malice (schadenfreude). Laughter is an ambiguous phenomenon, but in the present study it is most often related to humorous episodes in the narratives of interviewees.

The deceiving game, ventriloquism and the work of controlling anger can each be seen as a means of handling conflict between feelings and feeling rules. In the same way, humour can be seen as a means of handling tensions and contradictions in academic life. The 'joker' is a prized role in social structure (Mary Douglas 1975), and humour is a prized competence in Academia. Some characteristics of this competence are identified here, followed by a closer look at some of the forms and functions of humour within the academic hierarchy.

Humour as Competence

Humour embraces the co-existence of contrasts and contradictions and relies therefore upon mental openness to, and distancing from, a given social reality. Humour is also dependent upon the absence of extreme emotional states (Ben-Ze'ev 2000). When we are very agitated or over-excited, we remain blind to the humorous aspects of a situation. Humour is thus culturally compatible with the feeling rules of Academia with respect to emotional neutrality, and it is cultivated in both formal and informal settings. One man, an assistant professor, has this to say about the use of humour in formal settings:

> Being able to tell an [amusing] anecdote while presenting a paper, now that is something that definitely wins points – in the way that points are accumulated in those sorts of situations. But then, it's a different kind of amusement, I think [as compared with humour in informal situations].

Another example of humour in a formal setting:

> I was in [name of city] for a conference, and, eh, I made people laugh at a funny slide (laughs). My presentation was at a strategically good time, right at the end of that day, and I had a joke at the end that made people laugh. Yeah, I could explain it here – but that would take too long.

A joke brings people together in shared laughter, but a joke can also be used as a means of exerting power. A PhD fellow says:

> There's another situation in which laughter is extremely important. I've noticed that – when someone is defending a PhD thesis – some funny quip can be used to fend off questions in a polite sort of way. A joke is cracked, and then it [the line of questioning] seems to fade away. We [PhD fellows] really need to learn how to do that, because it's extremely effective. If there's a weak spot somewhere, making a bit of a joke out of it is a great way of getting it out of the way before questions get too critical, you know? I mean, if they start digging into something you can't really defend, you can crack a joke about it.

A joke shifts the frame of reference, such that the opponent's questions seem inappropriate. The opponent risks a loss of prestige if he insists on pursuing his question further.

Humour confers prestige. However, not everyone is granted mastery of this competence. One man, an associate professor puts it this way:

> Well, I'm not sure how it is, but some people have a really good sense of humour and then there are others who are less inclined to see the humorous side of things. I know someone here in this building that has that problem. I'm not sure. You could say that he is just a bit too unsure of himself – so maybe he just can't be open to seeing the funny side of things. So when – you know, humour might be saying something or interpreting something in a surprising way or in different way to what's expected – but instead of laughing, this guy just gets suspicious, you know? I find that a bit annoying.

Seeing the funny side or allowing oneself to become the butt of others' humour requires a sound sense of self-esteem. On this point, one PhD fellow says:

> Self-irony is enormously important. I mean, you have to be able to play the clown yourself. In that sense humour is a little bit democratic – you offer yourself freely for the good of the community, you know what I mean? (laughs) So they can have a good laugh at your expense. I mean, people who won't do that, well they are seen as being just a bit too up-tight. They won't give away a bit of themselves. Then there are those that laugh at others without letting others laugh at them – that's being just a bit too pompous.

A sense of humour calls for mental surplus, which can be unevenly distributed in Academia. Apart from that, humour often has its target, and in that regard some people are only willing to laugh at others.

Research into humour draws a distinction between pure humour – the so-called standard joke, the humorous content of which is bound within its own universe – and the applied form – the spontaneous joke, which arises from and is bound to a concrete social situation. The standard joke is often told in formal settings, while the spontaneous joke arises within informal settings (Mulkay 1992).

The applied form of spontaneous humour contests and plays with the given social reality. The precondition for being able to play humorously with social reality, however, is that the perception of this reality is shared with others. Different groups have different positions in the academic hierarchy. They perceive academic reality from different positions, and accordingly they have different forms of spontaneous humour.

Interviewees in the present study describe episodes involving laughter, but generally without fully accounting for the content that had been amusing. This imposes some limitations on my interpretation of the functions of this humour. With this reservation, I now present 'ground floor humour' among PhD fellows and 'joking relationships' among assistant, associate and full professors, as well as some examples of the use of humour as a tool of leadership, sometimes in the service of discipline.

'Ground Floor Humour'

The term 'ground floor humour' is inspired by David Collinson's use of the term 'shop floor humour' in his research on social organisations (1992). The term is used metaphorically here to describe the form of humour shared by those at the bottom of the academic hierarchy, that is to say, PhD fellows. There are also common traits between the 'shop floor' humour described by Collinson and the humour that occurs among PhD fellows. Both groups use humour as a means of handling boredom and as a means of expressing autonomy, including the expression of dissatisfaction with and resistance towards working conditions and superiors.

The place of PhD fellows at the bottom of the academic hierarchy creates the basis for shared experiences and for collective emotion work. Whether the individual experiences of PhD fellows attain the status of being a shared social reality, however, is dependent on the extent to which a certain number of them can meet, exchange experiences and negotiate their way to a shared definition of that reality.[1] In the present study, these preconditions were best fulfilled among PhD fellows at the faculty of health sciences, where there were many fellows. They were working within a shared scientific paradigm, met each other or worked together in laboratories, lunched together, experienced similar frustrations about laboratory tests that did not work out as expected, and all of them were familiar with frustration and fear provoked by temperamental professors and project managers. Here are some examples of these PhD fellows' descriptions of laughter and humour:

---

1 Social reality is a social construction that is created and negotiated. For a more detailed discussion of humour and social realities, see Fox (1990).

> Yeah, well I'd say we have a good laugh every day in the laboratory. It happens a lot. Well, actually, it happens every day. Jokes are cracked all the time, so there's a lot of grinning and a good deal of hilarity. We have a number of smaller laboratories and some of the lads are in one of them and we sit cracking bawdy jokes all day long (laughs). Not because we're all (laughs) that bad (laughs), but it's really good if one is able to let off a bit of steam, get away from it all one way or the other – because I've just become a dad, and my whole world has suddenly become so damned practical. It's really good when one can just be impulsive and have a good laugh.

Expressions such as 'some of the lads' and 'bawdy jokes' contests the emotional culture of Academia, which is elevated above gender distinctions and sexuality, such that this challenge also provokes laughter in the interview situation.[2] And:

> We also have a lot of episodes with ice fights in the corridor. We start throwing ice and racing after each other. We have spray bottles all over the place here. Something gets sprayed, and then something else happens, and suddenly there's a fight on.

This unconventional use of equipment and space in the laboratories can be interpreted, in the words of Mary Douglas, as 'an awareness of form against the formless' (1975: 93). The conventional use of spray bottles is contested by means of the ice fight. The ice fight itself undoubtedly provokes laughter, but the unauthorised use of spray bottles probably also contributes to the hilarity. According to this PhD fellow, these episodes contribute to a feeling of togetherness among the contestants. Another PhD fellow, a woman, is asked about laughter and she responds:

> We do that a lot [laugh] in the lunch pause and when we're sitting around running tests. I think we're very, very good at it. We laugh about private things and academic stuff, or just a funny remark, a joke – we're experts at telling dirty jokes at the lunch table. It can be all kinds of things. And it's not all just a long laugh. I actually think we're good at sitting and chatting about more serious things too. It's simply that we're all good friends in one way or the other.

They have lunch together, they work together, and they have fun together. They laugh at dirty jokes, but they also laugh about many other things – both from their academic and private lives. PhD fellows describe a culture of humour in the form of both standard jokes (often dirty jokes) and spontaneous funny remarks arising from the concrete situation or topic of conversation. By means of these forms of humour, boredom is handled as well as frustrations with academic work

---

2   Jokes, according to Zijderveld (1968) are not quite so natural and spontaneous as they may appear. On the contrary, they are closely related to the dominant values in society.

or temperamental professors. PhD fellows from the health sciences, however, were by no means the only PhD fellows to describe a sense of togetherness arising from shared laughter. As noted in Chapter 3, the counter-culture represented by some groups in Academia can also function as a community of humour. In an earlier excerpt a PhD fellow from the social sciences describes how the members of her study circle 'laugh a lot together' (see Chapter 3). While the source of this amusement is not made clear, it is indicated that some of it arises from the contrast between the conventional conception of science, which excludes emotional involvement, and the group celebration of emotional involvement in their own research. It is this contrast that releases laughter, a feeling of togetherness and a sense of gaining a position of strength as a group in the face of the conventional conception of science in the department. The following is an example of the spontaneous form of humour that challenges the academic hierarchy.

> When we started as PhDs there was a very authoritarian style of leadership – a culture that was strong on regimented discipline. We had a lot of fun playing with the idea that we would stand up at a departmental meeting and – since our salaries are fairly low – we would offer to do the cleaning in the evenings on the grounds that it would pay well! We had a great laugh about that idea when we were on our own – a kind of plebeian humour.

This idea can be interpreted as a humorous critique of the academic hierarchy with particular reference to the position of PhD fellows as being subject to authoritarian leadership and – in their view – on 'fairly low' salaries. This joke is one that pokes fun at the values of Academia by suggesting that they should do the cleaning since their labour costs would be cheaper than those of the cleaning staff.

Spontaneous humour among PhD fellows arises in informal settings and expresses disrespect for, or pokes fun at, the academic hierarchy. This form of humour can have its dangers. An assistant professor describes an episode that had taken place when he had been a PhD fellow:

> [It was] at a conference – the day after – and there was a very relaxed atmosphere. I cracked a joke. I can't remember what it was, but I said something funny, and the professor said something along the lines that it was a very good thing I happened to be in a place where the hierarchy was not present – or something like that, you know what I mean? I don't think he was trying to rebuke me exactly, but it's the clearest memory I have of feeling:" Well, OK, you need to be careful about what you say." But of course there are loads of things I joke about with people on my own level that I wouldn't dream of joking about in a more public situation, because there are a lot of very well-functioning hierarchical patterns – also in a place like this.

'You need to be careful about what you say', and since there are hierarchical patterns everywhere, some jokes are reserved for one's peers and for informal settings.

The position of PhD fellow gives access to 'ground floor humour' and to certain communities of laughter. As expressed by a relatively newly-appointed associate professor:

> Yes, there's a liberated kind of atmosphere [among the younger PhDs] and I was part of it one or two years ago, when I still had a lot of friends among the post docs and PhD fellows. We had something in common, so we could chat and grin together a lot and go out together. So that's what we did. There isn't that feeling of togetherness among the associate professors. No, I don't think there is at all. We don't really laugh together that much.

The PhD fellows' 'ground floor humour' is a tool that helps them to handle the feelings and frustrations that arise from both research and the power hierarchy, and this humour has subversive aspects in the sense that PhD fellows make fun of authorities, power structures and academic values.

'Joking Relationships'

The position of assistant or associate professor entails an individualisation and specialisation that lay the foundation for new kinds of collegial relationships. Unlike PhD fellows, one enters new social coalitions that are based on other criteria than shared rank at the bottom of the hierarchy. This does not mean that humour and laughter disappear, but rather that they take on a new social form and content. Humour becomes a particular style of communication between the persons selected to compete and to cooperate in Academia. Here are some examples of the ways assistant and associate professors describe this form of communication. One man, an assistant professor, puts it this way:

> Cheerful bantering is a daily event. For example, I've just been over to tease one of my friends, who has been trying in vain – no, I'm not sure it's in vain – but he's been doing what he can to get me to vote yes [to a particular policy]. I enjoy teasing him too. It's an amusing kind of banter. Yes, I think that happens all the time.

The interviewer asks who he jokes with in this way and he answers:

> With the people I think of as good friends. But there are also many I wouldn't dream of joking with in that kind of way. There are lots of people I'm not necessarily that fond of in here, but I just keep out of their way. That sort of joking banter happens between friends – that occurs to me now when we're

talking about it. Unfortunately, my everyday life isn't one long party in that kind of way. So, for me, the thing that matters is that there are some people I like, enjoy being with and know well in that kind of way.

This assistant professor describes a teasing, bantering form of humour between colleagues who like each other. This particular form is generally emphasised by men as being a prized form of masculine communication. Another associate professor, also a man, expresses this point in the following way:

> If fun and games are a feeling (laughs), I'd say that some of the men I'm most in contact with in the department actually find it much easier to enter into, than some of the women do. I suppose there are more men in this [academic] sector, so maybe that makes the competition harder. Not that I think women are assessed differently in terms of their objective qualifications – at least, I've never come across that kind of thing in any of the contexts I've been in. But maybe it's harder for them to have got as far as they have, and maybe that's why there are more of the women who seem to be, well, a bit tense. With them, you have to be a bit more careful about kidding them about something or other they've said than you do with male colleagues. I've run into that several times. They get really pissed off. I don't run into that problem in the same way with the men.

It is men that enter into this form of humorous communication. This point regarding a masculine form is developed further in the following exchange with another associate professor. The interviewer asks whether he and his colleagues often tell each other funny stories that provoke laughter, and he answers:

> IP: Yes, yes, and then we twist things that have been said! There are a couple of people who are really good at that. We often tease and kid each other a bit during coffee breaks, you know?
>
> I: As regards that kind of teasing and kidding, is it your impression that there is any difference between the men and the women?
>
> IP: Well, yes, that – that kind of carry on is "men only"!
>
> I: Men only?
>
> IP: Yes.
>
> I: You say that very emphatically?
>
> IP: Yes, ah, well, ah (pause), ah, that sort of thing, making wisecracks and teasing by twisting what people say, that kind of stuff belongs on the "men only" side.

Making wisecracks, kidding, twisting what was said or responding in unexpected ways, are ways of teasing and making fun of each other. This form of communication can comprise standard jokes, but more often takes the form of spontaneous jokes. During the interviews, this form of communication was also illustrated in practice by men, who sometimes added a politically incorrect statement followed by laughter. Here are some examples of statements that overstep the norms and are followed by laughter. An assistant professor says about a major piece of work he is on the point of completing:

> IP: So I'll be finishing it up within the next 14 days – and then, I'm looking forward to feeling proud!
>
> I: OK, that sounds nice! (shared laughter)

This assistant professor had explained earlier in the interview how inappropriate it is to indicate any feeling of pride, such that ventriloquism is a more discrete and appropriate means of expressing this feeling. By openly stating that he is looking forward to feeling proud, the assistant professor contests and plays with the norms that forbid the expression of feelings of pride. The contradiction between rules of expression and the expressed feeling releases shared laughter. Here is another example:

> I suppose this will continue [people in power deciding whether one is qualified to advance upwards in the hierarchy] – it's also the professors who decide whether or not you are professor material, if that's the way you want to go. Still, I hope I don't go around scratching too many backs (laughs).

This statement oversteps the norms of Academia in the sense that the assistant professor admits his career ambitions and also a willingness to scratch the backs of some superiors in order to get there. This contradiction between academic ideals and bleak reality is legitimated and released by laughing. A further example of poking fun at academic ideals is the following view, expressed by an assistant professor:

> Well, I don't think there's anyone in this system that isn't stressed to some extent or other. But I hope it gets better when you no longer have to take that external competition into account [due to gaining tenure]. Then you just have to live up to the level of the bare minimum for not being pointed out as a trivia-researcher (laughs).

This man contests the academic ideal of striving to undertake research of the highest calibre by defining his level of ambition as being just above the level of 'trivia' research. When the interviewer later asks about envy, he answers:

> IP: No, now that is completely unknown to me. I can't even think why you might suggest otherwise? (laughs)

At issue in this instance is an ironic rejection of any familiarity with envy, followed by laughter. He then describes how he can be pleased about the success of his foreign colleagues for the following reason:

> In cynical terms, they absolutely do not represent any threat in the direction of taking my associate professorship later on (laughs). Whereas, even with good friends, it's sometimes hard not to think: "Oh shit, did they do that!" Because then you have to try even harder yourself – "Oh no, I didn't get enough published last year, now I have to do even more" – you know what I mean?

In both of these excerpts the assistant professor can be seen to play with a juxtaposition of incompatible perspectives: the friendly relationships between colleagues and competitive relationships in which one person's success is the other's relative failure. He admits his envy, contesting thereby the feeling rules of Academia, and laughs.

In the last excerpt, the assistant professor points to the hidden antagonistic relationships between colleagues at the assistant, associate and full professor levels. These antagonisms arise from the logic of competitive relationships. The teasing, playful form of communication among assistant and associate professors can be interpreted as a humorous mirror image of competitive relationships in Academia. The antagonism, which is in fact present, is expressed and released in a competitive, playful form by means of teasing banter, twists of meaning and remarks that are not politically correct. These interactions were found to take place in dyadic relationships or micro-cultures. Several interviewees describe this form of communication as one of 'joking', and I have therefore termed it 'joking relationships'. In functionalist anthropology, the concept of 'joking relationships' refers to the form of teasing interaction in which friendliness and antagonism are combined (Radcliffe-Brown 1952: 91). Precisely this type of relationship accounts for a significant proportion of the form of humorous communication I have termed 'joking relationships' in the present study. 'Joking relationships' train actors to function in the competitive structure of Academia, while at the same time negating it by laughing. This form of humour is first and foremost described by men in assistant and associate professor positions.

Humour as a Tool of Disciplinary Leadership

'Ground floor humour' and 'joking relationships' can be interpreted as ways of handling emotional tensions on the part of different groups in Academia. The distinguishing feature of these forms, as compared for example to ventriloquism and the deceiving game, is their function of creating feelings of togetherness, solidarity and fellowship among equals. However, humour and laughter can also be used to promote solidarity and fellowship between superiors and their subordinates. Humour can be a tool of conflict resolution in a situation in which people who occupy different positions in the organisational hierarchy are brought together to face a common problem (Coser 1960). Humour releases shared laughter, which thereby confirms shared values. By means of humour, differences between people are negotiated and surmounted. Although it is to be noted that the meaning of humour – that is to say, according to Pizzine (1991), the content that actually amuses – should always be interpreted in the light of social relationships: who produces the 'joke', who is the object of the humour, and what are the relationships between those present?

Humour as a tool of leadership is most often used in formal settings, in which superiors and subordinates are brought together. In Academia, there are hierarchical relationships at many levels: between students and teachers, between PhD fellows and supervisors, and between academic staff and heads of department and directors of studies. Humour as a tool of leadership is not reserved, therefore, to any one level of the academic hierarchy, although one might well suppose that persons at the top of the academic hierarchy are more frequently in a position in which this possible means of handling the situation presents itself. The following are examples of humour as a style of leadership. An associate professor says:

> It is characteristic of my style that you have to take the rough with the smooth. So I can be very tough, also in terms of the way I choose my words, especially if I am provoked. But I do think that I quite deliberately – or at any rate, often in practice – coat my demands with a bit of humour in order to make them go down more easily. Yes, I think that's what I do.

Humour takes the sting out of this man's demands because it paves the way to a shared experience of humour in the situation and thereby to a feeling of fellowship, despite the hierarchical relationship between the giver and the recipient of those demands. Another associate professor says about a professor:

> The top scorer is our professor. He laughs a lot, and it's so infectious. He can lift the mood at a departmental meeting from being all the way down in the dumps – just one joke and his own hearty laugh, then suddenly the atmosphere gets lighter. I really admire that. I think it's partly just his nature to be that way. He quite simply can't help it. But there's probably an element of strategy in it too. I think he knows that he can lighten the mood that way.

The associate professor is uncertain whether this use of humour is strategic or otherwise, but nevertheless makes the point that a joke and an infectious laugh can be used to release tensions and raise the mood from being 'down in the dumps' at a departmental meeting.

The following excerpts illustrate ways in which humour can consolidate a feeling of fellowship between teachers and their students, but at the expense of persons who give rise to amusement by failing to live up to shared values and who thereby involuntarily become its target. An associate professor describes this scene:

> The students often find it hard to arrive on time, which is irritating – not just for me, but also for the others present. I am very strict about arriving on time, unless a train is delayed or something like that. When they are late, I get angry. My tactic is that I interrupt my teaching and bid them [the late arrivals] welcome. I interrupt what I'm saying and I say, "Now we must ensure that there is a chair for so and so. Are you sitting comfortably? Get your books out. We're happy to wait for you." It's not said ironically, but of course that is the way they take it up. And it keeps down the numbers that arrive late!

The teacher uses the late arrivals to create a sense of fellowship between himself and the students who have arrived on time, on the supposition that punctuality is a shared value. His humorous or ironic exposure of late arrivals releases laughter and a sense of fellowship among the punctual students, but also a feeling of relief that they are not its victims.[3] The next excerpt illustrates the way in which another teacher employs humour to discipline behaviour that she finds disturbing and destructive on the part of some of the men in her class.

> There was a particular group of guys [who behaved in a destructive way during teaching], so at one point, when this had been going on for a whole morning, I finally asked: "What would you call [man's name] if he were a woman?" And then one of the young women replied on behalf of the students: "We would say he was premenstrual (laughs), because he's always in such a mouldy sulk." This was her way of tackling it. I would never have dared to be so personal. The women had a great laugh altogether because, ah, well, suddenly that destructiveness, which we all felt that [man's name] and his cohorts had been displaying, was given a name.

This is a spontaneous joke that releases laughter and a sense of solidarity between the teacher and the women in her class, while the 'destructive' men among the students are ridiculed and disciplined. A final example illustrates the way in which involuntary mistakes on the part of a student can create a sense of fellowship between the other students and their teacher with regard to academic etiquette. The teacher in this case is also a woman, an associate professor, who says:

> There are many things that do that [make people burst out laughing]. It can happen (smiling) when someone involuntarily says something that is comical while they are presenting something or other – and perhaps they don't realise it at first. Then, when they do, it can be really quite funny, you know? It could also be something like, ah, like someone who has been given the role of critic, and who starts to make passionate comments about something, and then suddenly they see themselves as

---

3   It can be hard to draw a line between humour and irony, since both are based on saying the opposite of what is expected, such as the teacher who pays exaggerated attention, 'honour' and consideration to the late arrivals among the students.

having taken on the role of agitator, and they start to back off – you know what I mean? That can often give some really, ah, funny situations.

The students can step out of line in different ways. They can say something wrong or overplay their roles. Such episodes can be embarrassing, but, due to the simultaneous presence of form and bad form can also release laughter. The person who makes the mistake is momentarily made the target of humour, while at the same time a sense of fellowship between teacher and students and their shared confirmation of academic etiquette are strengthened.

Humour can be used a tool of leadership between superiors and subordinates at all levels in Academia. It can bring actors together disregarding their positions in the hierarchy, but sometimes also makes some of them the victim or target of that humour. 'Ground floor humour' and 'joking relationships' can also have their targets, but this aspect is highlighted most clearly when humour is used as a tool of leadership.

Summary

Humour arises from contrasts, contradictions and inconsistencies. The philosopher, Koestler (1964), defines humour as being 'in its essence a simultaneous orientation to two or more inconsistent perspectives', while the English anthropologist, Mary Douglas (1975: 93), describes 'the joke [as being] an awareness of the contrast between form and formlessness' and as comprising 'a play upon form'.

The contrast between form and formlessness or, in Koestler's words, the juxtaposition of inconsistent perspectives, can give rise to dismay, contempt and anger. Humour is characterised by interpreting such juxtapositions as being amusing, funny and liberating. Humour triggers laughter – a phenomenon that Mary Douglas describes as being cathartic, Sigmund Freud (1922) as being a manifestation of the unconscious, and the American psychologists, Nathanson (1992) and Tomkins (1962), as expressing a release from tension. Spontaneous jokes or applied humour arise from the tensions and paradoxes of social structure. Douglas speaks of 'the joke in the social structure' (1975: 98) and of spontaneous humour as comprising 'the juxtaposition of a control against that which is controlled, this juxtaposition being such that the latter triumphs.' (1975: 96) The strong connection between the joke and its social context gives spontaneous humour an important role in the study of organisations (Hatch and Erlich 1993).[4]

The social structure of Academia provides a basis for a range of emotional tensions that need to be handled. 'Ground floor humour' among PhD fellows, 'joking relationships' among assistant and associate professors and humour as a tool of leadership are seen here as humorous ways of handling the contradictions

---

4   Hatch and Ehrlich (1993) use humour as a guide to identifying paradoxes and conflicts in organisations.

related to different positions in the academic hierarchy.[5] These humorous ways of handling such contradictions reflect these positions, and can be differentiated from each other with regard to their social form, their object and their function.

Mary Douglas argues in her research regarding humour that the joke is always subversive with regard to hierarchies and control, while the English social anthropologist, Radcliffe-Brown (1952), argues that humour first and foremost has the function of promoting social integration by means of releasing tension, which facilitates acceptance of social reality. It remains unclear whether humour and laughter among different groups in Academia merely functions as a safety valve for releasing emotional tensions and promoting feelings of fellowship, or whether this humour and laughter also functions as a basis for contesting the prevailing social structure. The analysis presented in this chapter would support the claim that humour among equals has both integrating and subversive functions, while humour as a tool of leadership mainly serves an integrating function.

Humour is a prized competence in both formal and informal settings in Academia. Standard jokes and spontaneous humour confer prestige and recognition. Different forms of humour co-exist with a number of other ways of handling the tensions of academic life (the deceiving game, ventriloquism, anger management, etc.) Compared with the latter more individualised ways of handling feelings and emotional tension, humour appears to be a more generous and constructive means of handling such tensions. By means of humorous definitions of the tensions and contradictions of life in Academia, negative feelings are replaced by positive feelings of enjoyment, fun, relief and fellowship, which in turn yield a basis for collective awareness of and distancing from these contradictions. However, the precondition for such humorous definitions is that people do meet and talk to each other, thereby constructing a common definition of social reality, which in turn can become the object of such humour. This precondition is poorly fulfilled in many academic research environments in which individual academics work in a secluded fashion, buried up to the eyes in their own particular research projects and teaching assignments.

---

5 For a more detailed discussion of humour as a tool for handling one's own and others' emotions, see Francis (1994).

Chapter 7
The Academic Lunchroom

Connecting and Dividing Processes

Academia produces divisions between people, but also has some democratic features. This is the case in the formal sense that positions are attained on merit, rather than being dependent on social background or gender. Also all academic employees, in principle, have the right to contribute to scientific discussion. Connecting and dividing social processes are unfolded in formal contexts such as the research seminar, the assessment committee, the conference, and in informal settings such as chance encounters and meetings when employees collect their post, make coffee, stop up at the printer or sit down to lunch. Among these settings the lunchroom is highlighted in many narratives. The social structure of the lunchroom is discussed in the following, drawing on the theories of Simmel and Goffman. Thereafter, based on the narratives of the interviewees, it is shown how the lunchroom produces feelings of fellowship, processes that generate awareness of hierarchical distinctions and, finally, forms of social interaction in which both of these processes are present and, so to speak, reconciled.

The Lunch as Social Form

The luncheon venue in modern companies and organisations, at least in principle, is a space in which staff members are brought together on seemingly neutral territory, disregarding divisions of rank. This notion of supposed equality is made manifest by the provision of a staff canteen or communal lunchroom.[1] Why is this notion of convivial interaction between equals associated with meals? The question was answered by Simmel in his classical article on the 'Sociology of the meal' (1997). In his view, the meal is a particularly expedient means of generating fellowship between people who may not otherwise have any interests in common, but who can nevertheless achieve a sense of togetherness through their common participation in the ritual of the meal. According to Simmel, this fellowship-generating characteristic of the meal arises from the fact that eating is a physical human necessity. At certain intervals, we all need food. This common destiny gives rise to common actions, from which meal gains its social

---

1 Within the literature on the sociology of the meal there has been focus on the family meal and in particular the decline of family mealtimes. There are only few analyses of meals at the workplace, see also Holm (2001).

form. 'The sociological structure of the meal emerges, which links precisely the exclusive selfishness of eating with a frequency of being together with a habit of being gathered together such as is seldom attainable on occasion of a higher and intellectual order.' (Simmel 1997) The shared meal thus gains a supra-personal significance, which is expressed in aesthetic norms and rules of conversation. In this article, Simmel speaks of a community of individuals who do not have any particular interests in common, but he does not further explore the social character of this community. He does pursue this issue in another article, entitled 'Sociability' (1950), in which the democratic structure of sociability is emphasised. Moreover, he also emphasises the fact that this democratic character can only be achieved within a given social stratum: 'Sociability among members of very different social strata often is inconsistent and painful' (Simmel 1950: 47).[2] On the same point, Goffman (1967) speaks of role conflicts that arise in organisations when people of different rank are brought together in the elevator or in the canteen. Role conflict regards the incompatibility of egalitarian rank in one setting as compared with rank based upon position in the organisational hierarchy, and this conflict provokes discomfort and embarrassment. It would seem that both Simmel and Goffman support the view that the inclusive character of the meal is subject to some limitations.

According to Cas Wouters (1992), the 20th century has been marked by a process of democratisation that has promoted greater equality and informality in social relationships. It might be expected therefore that this process of 'informalisation' has also promoted greater ease in informal interactions between different groups: stewardesses and customers, employees and employers, professors and PhD fellows, etc.

PhD fellows, assistant, associate and full professors meet in formal and informal settings. Nevertheless, Academia is an individualised world in which people often work alone on their research projects and teaching assignments, such that being together with colleagues is not an integral part of the work process. Rather, conviviality is often subjected to careful – sometimes strategic – consideration and is thus not something that can be taken for granted.[3]

The qualitative data collected in the present study suggest that only very few departments have a communal tradition whereby all groups, disregarding rank, meet regularly for lunch. However, there are lunch traditions within distinct groups – first and foremost at the bottom of the hierarchy, that is among PhD fellows and post docs. Some associate professors lunch together, while others indicate that they wish they did have a tradition of lunching with colleagues. However, a number of those in permanent positions also appear to refrain from having lunch with their

---

2 My colleague, Christian Stenbak Larsen, has drawn my attention to the obvious links between Simmel's article 'Sociology of the Meal' and his later article on 'Sociability'.

3 It should be noted that my study is based on departments in which research is relatively individualised. See Chapter 1 regarding Becker and Trowler's (2001) distinction between rural and urban research environments.

colleagues. As one PhD fellow notes, 'Most of the permanent staff do not come to lunch,' followed by the additional comment, 'The least sophisticated ones do come.' This PhD fellow interprets the absence of associate and full professors from the luncheon table as being motivated by a difference in rank.

Another PhD fellow describes a setting in which permanent members of staff do meet for coffee and sometimes for lunch, whereupon they mark out protective boundaries in relation to the PhD fellows:

> In our department, you can't participate in the conversation during coffee breaks – the permanent members of staff are sitting there with the empty chairs between their seats [thereby occupying the available space and excluding others].

PhD fellows generally perceive the absence of permanent members of staff from lunch as indicating feelings of superiority among associate and full professors. However, according to Simmel and Goffman, their absence can also be interpreted as a means of protecting themselves from the strenuous discomfort entailed in participating in a communal lunch, given its related normative requirement to engage in social intercourse without regard to rank. The lunchroom as a setting that generates feelings of fellowship is primarily described by PhD fellows, and it is accordingly their narratives that dominate the analysis of this process.

Fellowship in the Lunchroom

The theory of Collins (1990, 2004) regarding interaction rituals and emotional energy, provides an analytical framework for understanding feelings of fellowship in the lunchroom and is briefly presented here. Collins has developed a theory regarding the basic form of the solidarity-creating interaction ritual. This ritual includes the following elements: the bodily co-presence of participants, the delineation of boundary with regard other persons – such that all participants know who is included in and who is excluded from their group, common actions or shared focus of attention on a common object or activity, reciprocal awareness of the shared focus of attention, and finally, a shared mood or emotional experience.

The academic lunchroom fulfils the preconditions for successful interaction rituals. Lunch is held within a physically delineated space such as a canteen, a lunchroom with table and chairs, or as one PhD fellow says:

> We sit in a little space on the landing, where we have been granted the privilege of using a sofa group. We sit there when we're having a bite to eat, and the few smokers we have sit out there too when they're having a puff.

The lunch thus unfolds within a setting in which participants are co-present and their boundary is physically – sometimes, symbolically – delimited as regards non-participants. One example is the following story, told by a PhD fellow:

> It's quite funny when our Head of Department gets a bit annoyed with us [PhD fellows] sometimes – that's because we make quite a bit of noise and we stick together by ourselves. He wants to integrate us [into the wider circle of academics], but we don't want to be integrated! We want to take it easy and be cosy on our own. We have one coffee table that we think of as being 'ours' – though of course it really belongs to the whole department. He puts up a sign [to that effect on the table], and we immediately make photocopies and hang them up all across the rest of the wall. Then he starts telling us off, and then we immediately stick together. That's the way it goes.

Lunch is based on common actions – the activity of eating – but also upon particular norms regarding conversational activities. According to Simmel (1997), conversation during meals regards topics of general interest discussed with some degree of personal detachment. Conversation does not venture beyond such general and typical topics, and is not the place to expound upon highly individual or deviant opinions. This framework is set by the basic premise of the meal, as a physiological event that is shared in company. The following are examples of conversation in the lunchroom as described by PhD fellows.

> The lunchroom [is] a perfect example [of having fun]! You've doubtless heard that before. I mean, that's where people make ironic remarks about the Research Councils or the Minister of Education or just other researchers – but it's done in a positive atmosphere and as part of a relaxed and amusing conversation, and so on.

> We do that a lot [laugh] in the lunch pause, and when we're sitting around running tests. I think we're very, very good at it. We laugh about private things and academic stuff, or just a funny remark, a joke – we're experts at telling dirty jokes at the lunch table. It can be all kinds of things. And it's not all just a long laugh. I actually think we're good at sitting and chatting about more serious things too. It's simply that we're all good friends in one way or the other.

> We laugh about all kinds of stuff, especially the American presidential elections. We've spent a lot of time chatting about that – why they are so strange. One can also talk about things that happen at home – like your boyfriend saying something weird or maybe you've gone out to see a film. We talk about films a lot. Sometimes the professor comes out and plonks down with us. He's like that, you know? So he comes out and collapses on the sofa and tells us a funny story about his new house or about how he would like to make [a humorous invention]. So then we have a long pseudo-academic discussion about whether we want this invention or not in [the faculty]. So it's often just a lot of tomfoolery like that.

These excerpts illustrate the general norms of light-hearted topics of conversation, relevant for all participants, such as the Research Council, the Minister of

Education, the presidential election and new films. Stories from one's private life are admissible, but only to the extent they are transformed into an amusing anecdote of more general interest, such as when a boyfriend says something 'weird' or a professor tells a 'funny' story about his new house. Conversation moves on the level of general interest, rather than catering for individual needs and feelings. This is illustrated by the following excerpt. The interviewer asks whether private matters are also discussed at the lunch table, and a PhD fellow responds:

> Yes, but not only that kind of thing. Well, there are a few that do have a tendency to always sit talking about their children. But I don't think that it's that bad [a breach of conversational norms]. I think what we all mainly do is tell stories about what has happened the day before. We're all quite good at it. You see, we're a core group of people who have the same sense of humour.

This excerpt illustrates the fact that topics of common interest are what count and some topics fail to meet the criterion of arising from a shared social reality. This applies to the topic of children in this particular group, but it can also apply to certain forms of humour. For example, one PhD fellow notes:

> Some of the lab technicians are a bit older [than us] and they don't always laugh at the same things we laugh at.

Personal matters, conflicts and the expression of personal feelings, such as hurt or anger, are also out of place in the lunchroom. A PhD fellow, whose three-year fellowship was financed by private industry, describes how he had felt hurt by a conversation among PhD fellows in which the category of industrial fellowships had been denigrated. He had subsequently opted to raise the matter outside the lunchroom, and explained this option in the following way:

> Well, I think you need to be careful there [in the lunchroom], because I think, yes, because there are so many people there – it's a place where one develops that sense of common identity. I would only very exceptionally take up anything that is – what would you call it? Personal – more a personal matter.

Collins speaks of a shared focus of attention on a common object or activity. Alongside the shared object of ingesting food, these conversational norms serve to reinforce a shared focus of attention. This shared focus, according to Collins, also serves as the basis for a process of emotional contagion, whereby feelings become common to participants (whether the feelings at issue are those of anger, grief, elation or some other feeling). Simmel does not address the issue of feeling rules of meal-time conversation, as such, but he does indicate a norm regarding the need to maintain a feeling of light-heartedness. The excerpts presented here also indicate feeling rules regarding the propriety of amusement, tomfoolery, humour and laughter in the academic lunchroom. Moreover, shared laughter is emphasised by Collins (2004) as constituting the best example of the process whereby collective effervescence develops, such that participants become physically absorbed in that form of deep and fully synchronised social interaction, which generates feelings of solidarity. By means of these processes, the group itself becomes a focus of attention, a trans-individual construct that in turn impacts upon participants in the group. It is in this manner that the performance of an interaction ritual can generate feelings of belonging, of solidarity with the group, as well as emotional energy on the individual level with regard to feelings of confidence, elation, enthusiasm and agency.

It is primarily PhD fellows who speak about fellowship in the lunchroom. They are the new arrivals, and they view their workplace from the perspective of the newcomer hoping to discover some sense of belonging to a community. Perhaps this is one reason why the lunchroom is highlighted in their narratives. The point was expressed by one PhD fellow in the following way:

> Considering how fragmented a department like this is, the lunch break – that half-hour – is just so incredibly important for getting the whole place to hang together at all. What I mean is – what can one say – it is my impression that it's important to have the chance to talk together and to laugh together and all that sort of thing.

This PhD fellow indicates the importance of the lunch break to the life of the department as a whole. In the same vein, an associate professor describes his earlier experience in a different department where all employees, disregarding their position in the hierarchy, lunched together:

> We had that [lunch for everyone] where I was before. At twelve thirty, all those who had time that day had lunch together. You could spend a half an hour together, and in a way that was quite nice and enjoyable. Of course there are all kinds of mysterious things that go on around a lunch table like that. And both the academic staff and the technical and administrative staff were there, so sometimes the table split into two parts, depending on what you're interested in. But there is nothing like that here at all.

Lunches that disregard differences of rank are indeed possible, it would seem. However, as the associate professor points out, it is not always possible to surmount different social realities, such that topics of conversation become split up between different social groups. According to Simmel, the shared meal paves the way for an aesthetic feeling of community, a particular kind of bond between participants. Collins' theory of interaction rituals and the generation of solidarity and emotional energy further clarify the way in which the academic lunch, due to feelings generated in that setting, can attain a significance that extends well beyond the meal itself.

Hierarchy in the Lunchroom

In the excerpt above, an associate professor describes how conversation at a lunch table that embraces different strata of employees can separate into different conversational groups insofar as it does not prove possible to hold a conversation that is interests everyone. However, different conversational groups do not always emerge, since interaction rights are unequally distributed among social groups. Formally speaking, all persons in the lunchroom participate as equal members of the organisation. This does not entail, however, that the formal hierarchy is no longer in play – although it may well appear to be irrelevant in the lunchroom. In this informal setting, academic hierarchy can present itself in the form differential interactional rights, including the right to pass judgement on others, to arrive late, to ignore others, to be listened to, and thereby the right to determine the topic of conversation at the expense of subordinates. In that case, individuals of higher rank will have more interaction rights in that setting, which serve to confirm and emphasise their superior status, while individuals of lower rank will perceive themselves as having fewer interactional rights, given their awareness of inferior status.

A superior position in the hierarchy can present itself in the lunchroom in the form of assuming the right to determine the topic of conversation and to dominate that conversation at the expense of topics that all participants might deem relevant. The following examples illustrate ways in which those in subordinate positions perceive those in superior positions as employing their interactional rights to dominate the content and level of conversation in the lunchroom. One PhD fellow offers the following view:

> Well, in most cases I find that talking to my colleagues is boring and embarrassing. I mean, the lunches – for a long time we had lunch tables that were overwhelmingly boring. Because the only thing they talked about was small talk based on the tabloid headlines – and in a totally non-analytical and dogmatic way. That's because there were a few of those manly knights and not the more sophisticated ones – actually, they were the least sophisticated ones. They simply set the tone and took over [the conversation] completely.

She continues:

> When they were discussing that television programme, Big Brother – I've never had so much as a glimpse of it – when they were talking about it, my feeling was that this is embarrassing: the fact that relatively well-paid academics could sit there and interest themselves in that kind of thing and talk about it. Then there are the ghastly, reactionary remarks about gay people, immigrants and women and so on – I also find that almost unbearable.

The same PhD fellow develops her point:

There are also a few of my colleagues that don't have any private/public barrier. They just start talking about sexual issues or how their wives put them down in some way or another. And they just pour it all out, you know? I also find that embarrassing. Apart from the embarrassment, I definitely see it as dominating my life – trying to, anyway. They never ask me about my life. They couldn't care less about it. They just invade my space. Instead of holding an interested and interesting conversation about this department's future, about our common visions and about the research we're involved in, they just cover everything with all their personal garbage and prejudices, and what they saw on the telly yesterday, and dump it all over my life. I think it's enormously dominating and embarrassing, and it makes me angry. But I usually just shrug it off by making some funny remark or other.

As a final example, another woman, an assistant professor has this to say:

We have a professor here and he's a really affable guy who likes telling jokes. But they have a streak of chauvinism in them, so – an old feminist like me – I almost feel on the point of throwing up when I hear them. I can't stand it at all, and I think it's dreadful – here, in the 21st century – that he allows himself to say things like that, you know? It just shows that he hasn't developed one bit in the last 20 years. There are still a number of the younger women on the scientific staff and almost all of the technical and administrative staff, who are middle-aged women like me, who are MUCH too accepting of the things he says – "Oh, isn't he funny!" They are not at all able to see through that chauvinist demonstration of power that is always there in obvious ways and in small ways.

The lunchroom is a space for social intercourse, but it is also a space in which hierarchies are negotiated and demonstrated while appearing to socialise. It is clear from these excerpts that both the PhD fellow and the assistant professor feel humiliated and upset. They do not intervene, however, and the PhD fellow actually tries to save the situation 'by making some funny remark or other.' Subordinates may find the professor's chauvinistic jokes actually amusing. According to Pizzini (1991), however, subordinates usually laugh at superiors' jokes, not because they are irresistibly funny, but because the boss is telling them. Both the PhD fellow and the assistant professor describe feelings of disgust, anger and embarrassment, but they do not express these feelings. This would constitute a breach of feeling rules in the lunchroom and, moreover, they do not have the interactional rights to do so. Yet these feelings do not fade away once the lunch break is over. They continue to nag the persons involved and may influence a decision to withdraw from the lunchroom. Apart from the right to determine topics of conversation without consideration of the preferences of other groups, the interactional rights accorded to permanent members of the academic staff also include the right to criticise and denigrate 'subordinates'. The following excerpts illustrate this right as exercised by superiors and as perceived by subordinates. A PhD fellow says:

> Yes, well, it's that thing of shaking their heads, or turning away when other people are talking, or just staring in perplexed amazement while others sit chatting at the lunch table with those big dumbstruck eyes. Some people are good at indicating what they think, more or less clearly. The Head of department is pretty good at indicating clearly whether he's pleased or displeased or whatever you call it.

This excerpt lacks specificity, but nonetheless serves to highlight the fact that the Head of department assumes the right to pass judgement on others. In another excerpt, which we looked at earlier in a different context, an interviewee is describing the disparaging tone that associate professors adopt towards him. He says:

> We can also be in a banal situation like a coffee break when I say that an organism has such and such genes, and they are important for something or other. Then I'm told that I'm completely wrong and that what I said was utter bullshit. Then I just clam up, because I can see that what I said was rubbish. That's really embarrassing, just so incredibly embarrassing.

The dismissive reaction on the part of superiors to such *faux pas*, as pointed out by another assistant professor, is hard to take – one is simply 'ignored for the rest of the discussion', which carries on without one. These examples illustrate ways in which the academic hierarchy is brought into play in the form of interactional rights in the lunchroom. Some have the right to determine the topic of conversation over the heads of others, as well as the right to pass judgement on others. Some have the right to be heard, while others do not enjoy that right. On this point, an assistant professor says:

> But there are lots of other temporary members of staff that nobody ever listens to, no matter what they might have to say.

The lunchroom is an informal setting for social intercourse between people of high and low rank, but it also appears to function as a space in which academic hierarchies are demonstrated under the guise of socialising. Persons in subordinate positions wish to participate because they want to be part of the community. It is during lunch, however, that one's social standing is revealed. Do the other participants listen to one? Do they respond to what one says? When lunch is attended by both higher and lower ranking members of the academic hierarchy, it may develop into a parody of the norms of social intercourse. Disrespect for the social codex of the lunchroom among those of higher rank can provoke feelings of shame and anger among those at the bottom of the hierarchy. These feelings can lead to social withdrawal from the lunchroom or from the ideal of the communal lunch. Those in subordinate positions may also adapt to the hierarchical norms of differential interactional rights, dutifully laughing for instance at the jokes of their superiors.

As described by some PhD fellows, they may also take a strategic approach to the task of adaptation by restraining frivolous remarks, adjusting a tone of voice or by taking on the mask of the serious academic when their supervisors attend a coffee break or turn up in the lunchroom.

The Fusion of Hierarchy and Fellowship

Having illustrated the processes whereby feelings of fellowship are generated and awareness of academic hierarchy is consolidated in the lunchroom, some forms of social interaction that serve to bring these two processes together will now be considered. This entails re-visiting some material that has been presented earlier, while maintaining a new focus of analysis. We have earlier seen that feeling rules and other norms pertaining to the consumption of meals in company demand that conversation proceeds on a general level and in a light-hearted fashion. However, participants in the academic lunch do have a life and feelings outside the lunchroom. We shall look at some instances in which this life breaks into the lunchroom in ways that combine the generation of fellowship with a consolidation of hierarchical position.

According to Bourdieu (1975), recognition by one's colleagues is the reward of scientific research, but competitive relationships in Academia also entail that one person's success is potentially the other person's failure. This entails that proclaiming one's success would constitute a breach of the norms of conviviality. As one PhD fellow says:

> There's also an element of one-upmanship. I've written for [a magazine] a few times and probably published more articles than many of my co-students. But I know that isn't something you sit and brag about at lunch. You have to keep a low profile about things like that. You can't let yourself be spontaneously happy in Academia. You have to take some account of other people's situations the whole time.

Account must be taken of the vulnerability of colleagues if things are to proceed smoothly in the lunchroom, and this excerpt describes how people must keep their successes to themselves. In Chapter 4, ventriloquism was described as a culturally legitimate way of displaying pride in one's success. Ventriloquism entails that the speaker can tell a good story, preferably a funny story, that complies with the conversational norm of pursuing a topic of general interest, while at the same time managing to convey in an understated fashion the background information that one has given a presentation at a prestigious congress, received an important invitation or had an article accepted for publication, and so on. The interesting feature of ventriloquism is that it can generate fellowship by providing a shared focus of entertainment while at the same time it allows the speaker to position himself or herself as having achieved academic success. Not surprisingly, it emerges that ventriloquism is a favoured strategy in the lunchroom. However, the condition of its success remains: the ventriloquist must comply with the conversational norms of lunchroom by introducing a topic of general interest and not be seen as indulging in self-focused concerns. This point was clearly made by the assistant professor, who said:

> It has to do with choosing one's story, doesn't it? It's a matter of telling a story which is unusual and funny along the lines of 'a funny thing happened on the way to the baker's'. It's an anecdote of that type, and nothing else. It's not a big, pompous presentation about having achieved a breakthrough.

As he explains:

> It belongs to the code that one puts oneself in the background and then foregrounds something else – your material – that you use, so to speak, in the same way as a ventriloquist. This gives one the opportunity to say, "Isn't it interesting?" But at the same time one gets the opportunity to present oneself as the person who got the insight and now is presenting things in an order that makes the whole thing new and fantastically interesting.

A variant on the gift-giving theme is that of bringing a cake for afternoon coffee. As one associate professor says:

> In here, you would celebrate it [a success] by – if it was something that was really good, like for example if I'd got money for a research project – a good way to tell about the success would be by bringing in a cake, and then telling about it while having cake and coffee. Then everyone could sit and be pleased about it.

The cake functions in the same manner as the good story – it provides a focus on a common enjoyment, while digesting the news of their colleague's success. The good story and the cake thus mediate between and bring together connecting and dividing social processes in the lunchroom.

What have earlier been termed 'joking relationships' among men should also be seen in this context, given feeling rules regarding the importance of convivial amusement in the lunchroom. This form of humour on the part of assistant and associate professors presents itself as convivial banter that comes to the fore during lunch and coffee breaks. An associate professor describes this type of humour as follows:

> IP: Yes, yes, and then we twist things that have been said! There are a couple of people who are really good at that. We often tease and kid each other a bit during coffee breaks, you know?
>
> I: As regards that kind of teasing and kidding, is it your impression that there is any difference between the men and the women?

IP: Well, yes, that kind of carry on is "men only"!

I: Men only?

IP: Yes.

I: You say that very emphatically?

IP: Yes, ah, well, ah (pause), ah, that sort of thing, making wisecracks and teasing by twisting what people say, that kind of stuff belongs on the "men only" side.

This form of humour was interpreted in Chapter 6 as constituting a playful manner of dealing with competitive relationships in Academia, involving as it does a struggle for position, but also a game that signals some distance from the competitive work conditions of academic life. This form of humour among members of the permanent staff is also a form of social interaction that reconciles the processes of generating fellowship by playing word games while consolidating rank and relative position. It is enjoyed in the lunchroom, although largely confined to men. Ventriloquism and joking relationships both arise from the structure and culture of Academia, but also comply with the feeling rules and conversational norms of the lunchroom.

Summary

The meal is based upon the common physiological needs of human beings. As ritual, according to Simmel, the meal is an expedient means of generating fellowship among participants. In the wake of recent processes of democratisation, the social setting for lunch in modern organisations is materialised in the form of the communal canteen or lunchroom. This analysis of the academic lunchroom identifies social processes that both connect and divide participants. It is shown how the formal and hierarchical structure of academic life makes its presence felt within the informal setting of the lunchroom, but also how particular fellowship-generating processes and forms of interaction within social groups help participants to shoulder the emotional burden imposed by the structure of Academia. Social and emotional processes in the lunchroom take on a special character insofar as they arise from the tension between hierarchy and equality. It is within this particular field of tension that academic actors feel and negotiate feelings of fellowship, a sense of hierarchical distinctions and of relative social position. This renders the lunchroom in an important indicator of who one is and where one is placed within the academic organisation. As described in this chapter, the lunchroom generates particular emotional processes and can therefore be seen as an important, but overlooked, indicator of the emotional climate within companies and organisations, including Academia.

Chapter 8
Social Bonds in Academia

I have identified a range of emotions in Academia on the basis of the narratives of PhD fellows as well as those of assistant, associate and full professors, including fear, uncertainty, anger, envy, laughter and humour. What can such feelings tell us about life in Academia? In this chapter and the one that follows, sociological theories of emotions are employed in order to elucidate what these feelings – and the ways in which they are handled – can tell us about social relationships in Academia. These analyses are meta-analyses of material presented in the preceding chapters, and for this reason some of the excerpts already presented are re-examined from a new perspective. The theories drawn upon are briefly presented at the start of each chapter. The impatient reader is welcome to skip these introductory sections, although I am convinced that familiarity with the relevant theory will facilitate understanding of the interpretations that follow.[1]

The American sociologists, Thomas Scheff (1990, 1994, 1997) and Suzanne Retzinger (1991), have developed theory regarding the relationships between feelings and 'social bonds' and they regard particular feelings as indicators of kinds of bonds.[2] Before considering what the feelings described here can tell us about social bonds and the quality of interpersonal communication in Academia, Scheff's theory is briefly introduced.

Theory

Feelings are always at play in interactions between human beings. Any given interaction is not merely a communication of content, but also a communication of some degree of respect and deference or of the absence of these feelings. Respect or disrespect is usually communicated by non-verbal signals (a welcoming smile, a yawn, a vacant look) and is most often not consciously intended. Markers of disrespect evoke uneasiness and shame, while markers of respect evoke feelings of pride and well-being. Shame and pride are thus potentially present in all interpersonal interactions. Shame encompasses a group of emotional states that includes feelings of embarrassment, humiliation, unease and uncertainty, each of which indicates a felt threat of being rejected by the other person. Thus, shame

---

1 Aspects of the present analysis have been published in Bloch (2002a, 2002b).
2 The theory of social bonds was developed by Retzinger and Scheff. It is Scheff, however, who has continued to publish work based on this theory, so that I hereafter refer solely to him.

is of great importance as a signal in social interaction. However, shame is also a feeling that is taboo in our society. We do not speak about our feelings of being rejected because such an admission would collide with prevailing conceptions of the individual as being strong and autonomous. Shame therefore has 'low visibility' (both for ourselves and for others). It presents itself because we are social beings, but it is suppressed before it reaches our consciousness. This does not mean that the feeling of shame has disappeared. On the contrary, it continues its life in the form of *unacknowledged shame*. On this point Scheff has been inspired by the work of the psychoanalyst, Helen Block Lewis (1971), who distinguishes two kinds of unacknowledged shame. The first, '*open non-differentiated shame*' entails a feeling of unease that is not identified as shame, and which is expressed in self-deprecating remarks, disjointed speech and long pauses. The second, '*bypassed shame*' presents itself in more subtle ways and is hidden beneath rapid and/or condensed speech, in which a person so to speak takes flight from the feeling at issue. Unacknowledged shame serves as the basis for *spirals of emotion*, i.e. successive states of feeling that release each other. For example, unacknowledged shame often releases anger for the reason that it is more tolerable to feel angry towards another person than to feel rejected by him or her. The expression of anger, however can lead to further rejection by the other person, thereby giving rise to renewed feelings of shame, and so on. Unacknowledged shame thus has its own dynamic in the form of spirals of emotion that are played out beneath the surface of interaction, and which affect the course of that interaction. The feeling of shame is not as such the source of damaged social relations. Rather, it is unacknowledged shame.

Any given interaction maintains, enhances, repairs or damages social bonds. The concept of *social bonds* refers to the relationship between the self and the other, in terms of attachment versus separation, dependence versus independence, and loyalty to the other versus loyalty to the self. Scheff is inspired by the theory of Emile Durkheim (1952[1905]) regarding the character of solidarity and the distinction between egoistic and altruistic societies. He is also inspired by sociological theory of the family developed by Bowen (1978, 1988) with particular regard to differentiation between the individual and the group, by Buber's (1958) development of the concept of 'I-Thou' relationships, and by Norbert Elias' (1978) discussion of 'I-We' relationships. On this theoretical basis, Scheff distinguishes three forms of social bonds, as follows. 1) *Solidarity* is characterised by mutual respect and responsiveness towards both one's own integrity and that of the other. This form of relationship does not entail an absence of conflict, but rather a willingness to listen to one's own voice and to that of the other – even when conflict is at issue. A bond of solidarity is characterised on the psychological level by feelings of pride and well-being. 2) *Isolation* is characterised by ceasing to be receptive to the voice of the other. One avoids the other, no longer listens to the other, but hears only oneself. 'Isolation' entails being separated from the group and alienated from the other. This bond is characterised on the psychological level by feelings of unacknowledged shame and anger. 3) *Engulfment* is characterised by merging with and conforming to the group at the cost of one's own integrity. That is to say, contact with the self is broken, leading to alienation from oneself. This bond is also characterised by unacknowledged shame and is subject to shame-anger spirals for the reason that suppression of the self also presents a threat to the self. Finally, the concept of 'bimodal alienation' is introduced to characterise social bonds in which there is conformity to one's own group and, simultaneously, 'isolation' in relation to other groups. 'Bimodal alienation' is the most prevalent form of relationship in modern western societies (Scheff 1994).

Social bonds are about communication – about listening to oneself and one's own voice, and listening to the voice of the other. Communication can also be a matter of listening only to oneself and thereby being alienated from the other, or listening only to the other and thereby being alienated from oneself. Feelings of shame and pride are the immediate indicators of the character of social bonds. In order to determine the character of the social bonds at issue, the focus of analysis is therefore upon verbal and non-verbal markers of unacknowledged shame, anger and other emotions in any given communication.[3] These markers do not provide definitive proof of the presence of particular emotions. Rather, they are merely indicators, which in conjunction with the context and the development of a narrative (or other form of communication) can be interpreted as indicating that specific emotions are present.

Some examples will now be given of possible unacknowledged shame and spirals of emotion, followed by an analysis of the forms of social bonds between colleagues in Academia.

Unacknowledged Shame and Spirals of Emotion

Shame-anger spirals are described particularly clearly by interviewees in connection with peer reviews that are experienced as having been offensive. Disrespect gives rise to the feeling of being rejected. This feeling is taboo and so unpleasant that it is suppressed before it reaches consciousness. Instead, it takes the form of unacknowledged shame and anger. The following sequences, which

---

3   Retzinger (1991) has drawn up a list of verbal and non-verbal markers of shame and anger. Bloch (1996) has drawn up a list of markers of so-called 'positive' feelings. These markers are important elements in interpretations of the character of feelings and of social bonds. Examples of verbal markers of shame include tendencies to mitigating description and the employment of negative descriptors of the self. Examples of non-verbal markers of shame include stammering, mumbling, the use of filler words, long pauses, 'laughed words', rapid speech, etc. Scheff also includes the occurrence of personal pronouns such as 'I', 'you', 'we' and 'it'. Interviewees primarily use I-language, which Scheff interprets as a language of separation. Since this may be a consequence of the interview form, this latter aspect has not been included in the interpretations made in the present study.

have been presented earlier in Chapter 5, illustrate the presence of both anger and shame:

> I: Could you give an example of a time when you experienced some form of disrespect on the part of your colleagues or a situation in which you felt "put down" by any of them?
>
> IP: I sit on [a particular] committee, which is associated with a certain amount of respectability (15 seconds' pause). Well, there is another of my colleagues who wrote a very offensive review of my [book] that made me really angry and cross. You can see it as a form of disrespect, also because there isn't really anything you can do about it. That's just the way things are… (little forced laugh).

And:

> It's actually a very competitive environment. If you are rejected, which I have actually been a few times, you are really pissed off, disappointed and upset, and angry and all the rest of it.

In the last line of the second excerpt, this associate professor states explicitly that she is angry. In addition, the phrase 'pissed off' is used, which can be seen as a further indicator of felt anger. Shame is not mentioned, but the word 'rejected' in the first line of the second excerpt is a verbal indicator of the presence of shame.[4] The very long pause in the first excerpt may indicate non-differentiated shame.[5] Finally, the little forced laugh in this excerpt may be a further indication of unacknowledged shame. Here is another sequence:

> I: How did it come about that you have the position you have now?
>
> IP: Well, it's a bit of a dreary story (little laugh). I used to be a PhD fellow, and, ah (pause), they [the department] advertised an assistant professorship. So I applied, and I was turned down initially. But then the person who had got the job…ah… (rapid speech:) withdrew and (stammering:) I got in that way (little laugh). So it worked out in the end.

She adds, later in the interview:

---

4   Words such as 'rejected' and 'dumped' are included in the list of verbal markers of shame drawn up by Retzinger (1991).

5   A long pause is not necessarily an indicator of shame. For example, a long pause may be due to a need for second thoughts before responding to a question. It is the context of the response in conjunction with other indicators that constitute the basis for a concrete interpretation.

I could see from the assessment they [the assessment committee] made that they simply had not read my thesis. In my opinion, they hadn't treated my work fairly. They had just – well, it was my impression that they had made up their minds beforehand to say: "Yes, well, her field of work is not central enough, seen in relation to the tasks she would need to accomplish in this department." So I was really sour about it, disappointed, frustrated and all that kind of thing.

The first excerpt includes both verbal and non-verbal markers of shame. The phrase 'turned down' is a verbal marker, while filler words, pauses, rapid speech, stammering and nervous laughter are non-verbal indicators of unacknowledged shame. The self-descriptor 'sour' in the second excerpt can be interpreted as an indicator of anger, but also as a negative self-descriptor. Being 'sour' carries negative connotations of being discontented, sulky or embittered – as in the use of 'sourpuss' and 'sour grapes' as descriptors – and can therefore also be interpreted as a verbal indicator of shame.

The peer review constitutes a particular form of interaction. In Academia, the peer review is first and foremost conceived as an assessment. However, it never constitutes a purely objective assessment, since the tone of an assessment and the manner in which criticism is worded always communicates some degree of respect for and approval of the work under assessment or of disrespect for and disapproval of that work and thereby of its author. Moreover, other more readily concealed criteria can also be brought into play. The peer review, as described earlier in Chapter 5, can give rise to the experience of feeling disparaged and ashamed. The persons in these examples feel wronged and offended. They feel rejected, but they do not mention this feeling. On the contrary, we hear their anger, alongside a range of verbal and non-verbal indicators of shame. It is of course a question of interpretation whether these sequences should be seen as examples of shame-anger spirals that are once more brought into play in relation to remembered events. It was clear, however, that these interviewees were indeed strongly affected by their recollections of these past episodes, which supports the view that shame-anger spirals – presumed to have been activated earlier within the social relationships at issue – made their presence felt once again in recollections of these episodes.[6] Unacknowledged shame and shame-anger spirals significantly affect the character of social bonds and thus of communication between colleagues. The focus of this analysis will now be upon the kinds of social bonds in Academia.

'Isolation'

'Isolation' entails, as we have seen, that the parties involved no longer listen to each other. The offended person shuts off the voice of other person and only listens

---

6 The focus of the present study is upon structures of experiences. It must be emphasised that a temporal perspective is needed in order to provide full empirical evidence for the presence of recurrent spirals of emotion.

to his or her own voice. In the present study, 'isolation' manifested itself in one of two ways: either in the form of physical or mental 'withdrawal' or in the form of open 'warfare'. These two forms of isolation, 'withdrawal' and 'warfare', are based on different kinds of anger. The experience of 'helpless anger' is related to withdrawal, while 'explosive anger' – also termed the rage of humiliation – is related to the tendency to declare war. 'Withdrawal' and 'warfare' will now be illustrated. The following sequences, earlier seen in Chapter 5, illustrate the dynamic of withdrawal as a reaction to offensive peer reviews:

> IP: It [that review] was so nasty, on such a low level and so plain bad, that I would never take it up with him face-to-face – never!
>
> I: So, one doesn't do that?
>
> IP: I don't know. Other people – who've experienced the same kind of treatment from him – have given him a piece of their mind, but I couldn't be bothered having anything to do with it.

This excerpt illustrates the way in which the offensive reviewer is transposed in the mind of the interviewee to a being who is so abhorrent that the interviewee will have no further contact with him. Despite this effort to eliminate this reviewer from the universe of the interviewee, the use of phrases such as 'so nasty', 'on such a low level' and 'so plain bad' indicate that anger is still present. Here is another example:

> I complained to the editor and I also thought a good deal about writing to the person concerned. But the review was such a bad piece of work that it would be ridiculous to sit and write about it. It would just make the whole thing even more ridiculous, you know? I actually did make a few attempts at it last summer, until I found out that the only thing to do was just to let it wash away down the drain.

Here we encounter the anger of helplessness. The interviewee would like to take action, but finds herself powerless to do so. What emerges from this feeling is a categorisation of the review and reviewer as being 'ridiculous' and an intimation of its assigned status as garbage, expressed in the resigned decision to allow it to 'wash away down the drain.'

In these examples, 'isolation' from the other is achieved by means of a mental segregation of both the offence and the offender. This form of mental segregation may also be accompanied by physical withdrawal. Several interviewees report that disappointment and anger had contributed to a decision to physically withdraw from their departments in favour of what one of them termed 'kitchen-table-research' accomplished from home. Shame and anger are released when offence is given and taken among peers. Apart from these feelings, offensive behaviour on the part of those of superior rank towards subordinates can also generate fear, which in turn can give rise to physical withdrawal. As one PhD fellow comments on her reaction to an offensive assessment of her work during a so-called evaluation seminar:

> Yes, but I don't show up any more. I feel that someone may stab me in the back. I just pick up my post and then go home again.

'Isolation' by means of withdrawal is related to helpless anger. The offended party abandons the attempt to relate to the offending party, who is defined as being dangerous or abhorrent. The views of the other are not heard, the offended person hears only his own or her own views. This can give rise to a severe restriction of the social space of the offended party, sowing the seeds of the experience of loneliness.

Offensive assessments can also trigger explosive anger (the rage of the humiliated). Explosive anger constitutes a breach of academic feeling rules. This may be the reason why interviewees primarily attribute explosive anger to other people. However, explosive anger is by no means uncommon, as pointed out by one professor:

> Normally, my colleagues here are incredibly well-behaved – the same as at any university. They know how to restrain their feelings and are very analytical in their approach to things. But once in a while their feelings run away with them. I think I can safely say of all the colleagues I have known throughout the years here, that there are situations in which they blow their tops off. That applies to just about everyone – some situation or other arises in which the pressure becomes too much and one lets other people know it.

The following excerpt, parts of which have been cited earlier, but is here presented in its entirety, illustrates the way in which an offensive peer review can generate 'isolation' in the form of 'warfare' between the parties involved. An associate professor, who had acted as an assessor, describes his colleague's reaction to that assessment:

> He was extremely incensed and quite beside himself – running around showing the recommendation to all his colleagues. I had expected that I would just express my regrets and say how things had been, and so on. But it developed such that I had to virtually defend myself – physically, so to speak, virtually with my body (little laugh) – because I could feel how the situation was escalating. In the end he declared that he would not speak one more word to me again in his life. Since then – and that was [a few] years ago – he has looked right through me whenever we've met, and we have never said hello to each other. What happened since is that he's been trying to sabotage some of the work I have been doing to get this department on the right tracks. This has given rise to a great many quarrels within the department and a major personal conflict. It has had some deeply felt consequences that have also affected personal relationships in

> here. It has also led to a couple of episodes in which people really let fly and let off a lot of stream, including myself. Any cooperation with that person will probably never again be possible.

This excerpt illustrates the rage of the humiliated, but also the destruction of a social bond. Communication breaks down to such an extent that it almost reaches the point of physical violence when the conflict is at its height. In the aftermath, both parties cease to 'hear' the voice of the other, just as they express their mutual disrespect by failing to greet each other. The word shame is not mentioned in this narrative, although both parties have presumably – at different points in time – felt rejected by the other.

The following example is rather different. It does not concern an offensive peer review, but an associate professor who feels repudiated as a professional academic when his services as a PhD supervisor are rejected. The supervisor who is selected in his place describes the reaction of his rejected colleague in the following way:

> Then my colleague just totally exploded – it was indescribable. I've never in my life seen anything like it. It was extremely unpleasant. The rage lasted maybe only half an hour, but the aftermath – the bitterness, the suspicion, and then the accusation that I had been forging intrigues, which I had not done at all, and all that stuff – has been going on so long. And it has spread so much that – well, now we are talking about feelings, and that is what it's all about – the group has been infected by it. Because everyone knew that something was going on, and they probably know what happened too. I've told a few people myself, at any rate. So it has created a vigilant, careful sort of atmosphere. We all know very well from a pragmatic point of view that there has to be room for all of us here, but we don't give away an inch of ourselves – because we don't want everything to break down once again. We've all just been away at a seminar – all three of the parties involved [the PhD supervisor, the PhD fellow and the rejected supervisor] and others from the department went away together for a few days. We carried it off, just about – it was a year and a half, no, almost a year, since it had happened. It went OK. People put a brave face on things on the whole, but there were some that didn't speak to each other and that kind of thing.

This excerpt illustrates the destructive power of unacknowledged shame and also illustrates the interplay of spirals of emotion between two associate professors. The repudiated party explodes in rage directed at the successful associate professor, who feels rejected and presumably also angry about his colleague's reaction. Broken bonds are maintained insofar as the two parties do not speak to each other. Although a temporary ceasefire is indicated in the last part of this excerpt, it also clearly shows that a broken relationship affects other colleagues. This development creates a basis for 'bimodal alienation', that is to say, 'engulfment' within one's own group and 'isolation' in relation to other groups. 'Isolation' of this kind can be expressed in the form of recurring argument or conflict, but 'warfare' in a collegial setting can also proceed by means of more sublimated forms of aggression. On this point, an associate professor notes:

> Many academic debates [conflicts] are not conducted in the corridors; they are not conducted in the rooms or offices. They are conducted in newspapers. Sometimes you can read some really unpleasant things. They don't hold back because it concerns a colleague – quite the contrary, in fact.

Another assistant professor says:

> There are other ways of getting back at each other, or whatever you want to call it – of getting things out in the open… I mean, if one person has criticised someone else's research, they won't be on speaking terms for a long time. There won't be a quarrel, but the conflict will come to the fore indirectly when one of them writes a review, for example, which clarifies what it is all about.

The associate professors use urbane expressions such as 'academic debate' and 'criticism' of research, while at the same time it is clear that points are sometimes made in extremely unpleasant ways. Dialogue between colleagues is replaced by public attacks on one another's research, which can have the character of revenge.

Several narratives describe situations in which colleagues refrain from greeting each other. According to the theory of social responsiveness developed by the Swedish social psychologist, Johan Asplund (1987), the form of 'not-greeting' is a learned form of asocial unresponsiveness, which can be interpreted as constituting an elementary exercise of power. We deny the other's existence by means of the practised form of 'not greeting', and at the same time we also take from the other the capacity to acknowledge and confirm our own existence. The 'not-greeting' form is a strong expression of denying the other person a voice, laying the foundation for the unacknowledged shame of both parties, and thereby fuelling continued 'isolation' between them. Only few of the interviewees spontaneously report that there are colleagues with whom they are on terms of 'not-greeting'. Yet the majority of interviewees tell stories about others in their departments who never greet each other. These stories are expressed in remarks such as the following:

> Yes, there are some who don't say hello to each other. I know there are some who certainly do not greet each other.

One of the few to admit to being on 'not-greeting' terms with a colleague has this to say:

> There came a time when we no longer greeted each other, and I have a very strained relationship with (woman's name). I haven't said hello or goodbye to her in ten years.

The peer review, competitive relationships between colleagues and conflicts between rival groups of colleagues sow the seeds of disrespectful practices that evoke unacknowledged shame and persistent spirals of emotion. One fails to hear the other's voice and listens only to one's own (being alienated from the other). One does not show respect for others, hides one's own feelings and ignores those of others. Interactions of this kind can have prolonged effects upon the character of social bonds, paving the way for 'isolation' by means of withdrawal or by means of hostilities that alternate over time between phases of ceasefire and open warfare. As an assistant professor says:

> You're sitting there at a meeting and then, suddenly, it comes to the fore. One person says something and then a quarrel breaks out. Then they calm down again. It would be completely impossible for anyone outside the group to know what on earth is going on.

The social structures of Academia sow the seeds of 'isolation' in the form of damaged social bonds among colleagues. 'Engulfment' is another form of damaged social bond.

'Engulfment'

'Engulfment', as we have seen, is characterised by identifying with group norms to an extent that excludes one's own judgements, values and feelings. One conforms to the group at the cost of one's own integrity. In the same way as 'isolation', the bond of 'engulfment' gives rise to feelings of shame and unease because repression of the self presents a threat to the self. Academic life requires one to assimilate the prevailing values and norms, including the etiquette and unwritten rules of Academia. One may assimilate these largely unwritten rules in such a way that one's self becomes merged with conformity to them, or one may try to maintain some critical distance. 'Engulfment' occurs when one identifies with the voice of the group at the cost of one's own feelings and sensibilities. 'Engulfment' often occurs in conjunction with 'bimodal alienation'. In the case of 'bimodal alienation', one wholly identifies with group values and feeling rules, while distancing oneself at the same time from persons who do not master the values and codes of this group. The latter persons might be, for example, students, PhD fellows, new arrivals or women colleagues.

'Bimodal alienation', according to Scheff, is widespread in modern society. Academia as we have seen embraces a range of different communities, including cohesive groups among PhD fellows, groups that share a particular sense of humour, friendship groups and fellowship based on shared academic interests among those of professorial rank.[7] The individual member of any such community can become

---

7 Informal communities, brotherhoods and men's groups are well-known categories in Academia. Reference should here be made to Scheff's analysis (1995) of 'gang' or 'clan'

'engulfed' by the group or fellowship to which he or she gives allegiance. Some of the previously described strategies, by which tensions between feelings and feeling rules are handled, such as 'the politics of friendliness' and 'the deceiving game', are forms of interaction in which 'engulfment' and 'bimodal alienation' are readily brought into play. When we practice 'the politics of friendliness', we hide our anger and irritation behind a mere mask of friendliness towards others. When we play 'the deceiving game', we hide our uncertainty and fear of others behind a facade of certainty and control. In both cases, our own feelings are kept well hidden in order to conform to the feeling rules of Academia. Conformity of this kind, however, does not always eliminate feelings of unpleasant tension. We have seen in Chapter 4 that some assistant professors experience moral scruples regarding 'the politics of friendliness', just as some express reservations about willingness to play 'the deceiving game'. The experience of dissonance between group norms and one's own feelings can be overcome by means of unconditional identification with group norms, that is to say, with the feeling rules or 'etiquette' of Academia (cf. Ashforth and Tomuik 2000). Identification of this kind entails the process of 'engulfment'. The voice of the self is toned down in order to comply with the norms of Academia. The politics of friendliness and the deceiving game are each motivated by a desire to be accepted and to survive in academic life. These strategies can become taken for granted practices at the cost of repressing one's own immediate feelings. In that case socialisation to academic life has succeeded, but only at the cost of denying the moral signal-value of one's own feelings.

Solidarity

The bond of solidarity is characterised by the ability to hear both one's own voice and the voice of the other. This bond is related to feelings of pride, enjoyment and well-being. 'Ventriloquism' and humour can be seen as expressions of the bond of solidarity.

Pride is the feeling that accompanies recognition and most people experience joy and pride in the achievement of academic merit. Being invited to be a keynote speaker, having an article published in a prestigious journal or receiving a research grant are among the forms of personal recognition that may well reinforce a person's sense of solidarity with the research community and the academic world more generally. However, it is not acceptable to display one's pride to colleagues in Academia. 'Ventriloquism' is an acknowledged way to circumvent this norm. 'Ventriloquism' can be seen as contributing to bonds of solidarity insofar as the researcher maintains awareness of and contact with the forbidden feeling of pride, yet by expressing this feeling only in the manner of a

---

structures among professors. These fellowships have both material significance in relation to the allocation of grants, appointments and recognition of scientific work and emotional significance as fellowships of identity.

ventriloquist the researcher demonstrates respect towards the burdensome issue of competitive relationships among colleagues. By means of ventriloquism the proud academic can render his or her success visible to others, while at same time enriching listeners by telling a good story or by imparting some interesting piece of information. Social bonds are hereby maintained.

Humour can also be interpreted as a bond of solidarity. Humour has already been described as a means of relieving social tensions. Humour dissolves antagonism by means of shared laughter, in which all are acknowledged participants. Humour promotes the sense of togetherness, since all voices are heard when laughter is shared.

However, both ventriloquism and humour entail potential ambiguities with reference to social relationships. Ventriloquism can verge upon or develop into self-promotion, such that only one's own voice is heard. Likewise, humour often has a target. We laugh at other people, or we confirm our membership of one fellowship by targeting groups defined as outsiders. One assistant professor makes this comment about her colleague from the standpoint of an outsider:

> And then he sits there in the lunchroom cracking one sexist joke after the other'–
> and everyone laughs! Sometimes it makes me feel like throwing up.

Humour is by no means always inclusive. Laughter and humour can create solidarity, but can also be an expression of 'bimodal alienation', characterised by 'engulfment' within one group and 'isolation' with regard to other groups. The 'ground floor humour' of PhD fellows creates bonds of solidarity, but is also targeted at the world of Academia, professors, etc. 'Joking-relationships' among tenured members of staff also create solidarity, but can take the form of 'bimodal alienation' targeted at women.

'Nourishing and Wearing Relationships'

Based on Scheff's theory, I have sought to demonstrate some of the ways in which feelings and the prevailing culture of emotions affect the character of social bonds in Academia. But how do assistant, associate and full professors describe their own collegial relationships? As the closing question in each interview, all interviewees were asked to characterise their own social relationships at their place of work and their relationship to the academic world more generally. More specifically, they were asked to what extent they viewed these relationships as being respectively 'nourishing' or 'wearing'.[8] We shall now examine the ways in which these relationships are assessed by interviewees.

---

8   As noted earlier (cf. Chapter 2), these two concepts constitute a rhyming pair in Danish ('nærende' or 'tærende') and this dichotomy is a familiar feature of everyday discourse among Danes.

Most interviewees respond to this question with the claim that some aspects of academic life and some relationships are nourishing while others are wearing. The aspects most frequently emphasised as constituting positive and nourishing elements are research activities and the freedom to work in depth with research problems. The character of research as a passion comes to the fore in this context, and relationships that are seen as being academically enriching are mentioned, as are everyday contacts with closer and trusted colleagues and points of inspiration from the academic environment more generally. Interviewees tend to begin by considering the positive and nourishing aspects of their everyday working lives and then turn to consideration of the aspects they find most wearing. These concern relationships characterised by mutual indifference, lack of interest in each other's work, and an atmosphere at the workplace characterised in such terms as 'resigned', 'hostile' or 'warlike'. A tendency to describe the collegial relationships of everyday life as being 'damaged' in one way or another is especially pronounced among associate professors. These relationships are described by two men in the following ways:

> I was employed here for a very long time before anyone began to ask me, hesitantly, what my research was actually about... It's surprising how rarely one is asked about the research one is doing. It is simply unbelievable, just how rarely one is asked about it. I can imagine that out at [another faculty] it's even worse.

> I'd just like to go back to what I was saying earlier – one produces something [a paper, an article] and one doesn't get any feedback on it. It's a form of 'every man for himself' in a minor sort of way. You can't get away from the fact that people can not be bothered having anything to do with the problems – maybe they are up a slightly a different alley – that other colleagues are investigating. And, ah (pause), hmmm (slight cough), no, I wouldn't say that it's a form of disrespect – just a kind of inertia. So, ah, well, that is one of the things – I'd say it's virtually the only thing – that I miss in this department.

The latter associate professor wants to be 'heard', but nobody listens since his colleagues do not interest themselves in each other's work and cannot be bothered to use time on the work of others. His working environment is characterised in terms of 'every man for himself'. Others speak more generally of departmental environments in which one does not 'hear' the voice of others. Another associate professor says:

> Angry, I suppose I am. But – what do you call it – I don't know whether it is anger or – what do you call it – a general dissatisfaction with the mentality at the university, to which I have resigned myself. I wouldn't say that I stand there and get angry, so 'angry' doesn't really fit the situation. But that does not mean that I'm happy with it. It's more a matter of 'resignation'. I do not like the

atmosphere here in this department. But I cannot do anything to change it. The younger ones can do that. So, I prefer to use my energy on things that are going well, as I see it, and which I like doing.

'Isolation' begets 'isolation'. This associate professor channels her energy away from her colleagues. She no longer listens to their voices. Another associate professor describes his colleagues as not thinking of each other and being interested in each other as persons.

> Well, I'm one of the few that's in here almost every day. That means that the social life in here is next to nothing. It also means – as I said the day before yesterday, when you asked if I was going to lunch – that we don't do lunch here. It's a complete coincidence if you happen to run into someone else, who is also on their way to the canteen. So, then you might [have lunch together], but it isn't something you just do. There are just a few people one has contact with – with whom I have contact, in more academic contexts. So, in that way, we get to know each other a little more. One can ask how the children are and where one is going on holiday and that kind of thing – things that otherwise no one would know about. I think most people in this department would have no idea whether I ever go on holiday or whether I have children. That is often a bit frustrating.

He continues:

> Not a damn thing goes on in here – there aren't any collegial get-togethers. You're just here, and whether your children are sick or you're going off on a holiday, nobody knows a thing about it – except maybe your own students. So, in that way they [students] can help to fulfil that function as well.

This associate professor experiences a work environment in which collegial relationships are characterised by indifference and a lack of interest in each other on a personal level. This is clearly described by another associate professor who, when asked about his relationships with colleagues, responds:

> As regards that, I'm fairly indifferent. Well, it sounds a bit sinister to say 'indifferent', doesn't it? But in fact we have nothing in common in that sense – with my colleagues, not at all, no, nothing at all.

This form of passive indifference between colleagues changes character, however, when they encounter each other in settings in which feuds regarding the allocation of resources are played out. In these settings, 'isolation' takes on a different character. One associate professor provides the following description:

> And then the academic staff does hold meetings from time to time. But, well, there's nothing amusing about those. What you do see quite clearly are lines

> being drawn up and trenches dug out. Certainly, nobody goes in there to raise a laugh. If they do, it's usually a bad sign (laughs). Yes, well that's because it would be a matter of someone getting away with something or other – or something along those lines. So it [the laughter] would be scornful. So, it's not because it's particularly amusing. It damn well is not. What I mean is that's just the way this place is. There are groups that try to...

The fight may be fair, but many associate professors describe such meetings as being highly unpleasant and very tense. Another associate professor provides a more gentle description:

> Yes, well, in general I'd say that the tone of relations is reasonably friendly, but that is just the tone we are talking about now. As I've just been telling you, many of those who come [to these meetings] are egotistical in a fairly vigorous kind of way – as regards the way they try to play their cards.

This associate professor emphasises friendliness as the norm regarding everyday contact between colleagues. He draws a distinction, however, between the friendly tone of these relationships and the actual relationships that come to the surface during the struggle to gain resources. In these settings, cards are played with a view to maximising personal gain. There is no room to accommodate others, only one's own interests are at stake.

These excerpts paint a picture of Academia as a workplace in which colleagues do not listen to each other or take an interest in each other as fellow academics or as persons. That is to say, a workplace characterised by 'isolation'. This characterisation undoubtedly varies to some extent from one department to another. Moreover, one's position in the academic hierarchy also undoubtedly affects the ways in which these relationships are experienced. For example, PhD fellows and assistant professors most often describe relationships of this kind from the viewpoint of a spectator. As one assistant professor formulates this point of view:

> All that strategic shit and the plotting and machinations that go on up in the system – well, I can live with that, since there are so many other things I like about this work I have.

It is first and foremost the associate professors who describe 'isolation' among their peers.

Summary

Scheff's theory regards the character of social relationships and interpersonal communication, specifically the extent to which one 'hears' oneself and 'hears' the other/the group. Taking my point of departure primarily in the narratives of associate professors, I have identified the interplay between social structures, the prevailing culture of emotion, the feelings of academic employees and the character of social bonds. Using Scheff's theory as an analytical tool, I have illustrated the way in which particular emotional episodes can generate dynamic spirals of emotion that, over time, can have lasting impact upon the character of communication between colleagues. According to Waldron (2000), the most intense feelings in an organisation are those regarding social relationships among colleagues. These feelings have a vital influence upon labour relations and on the life of the organisation, but are overlooked in organisational research. Feelings provide an important analytical tool that can be employed when exploring and identifying the character of social relationships in qualitative terms. Scheff's theory has served this purpose in the present study.

Ehn and Löfgren (2004: 27) express surprise at the idea that a '…rational organisation such as Academia sows the seeds of personal and emotionally laden relationships to the extent it does.' My point, however, is that the character of feelings and social bonds in Academia are not expressions of personal dynamics, but that the social structures and prevailing culture of Academia constitute a stable foundation for the recurring and repetitive character of these feelings, and thereby for the character of its social bonds. On this basis a hypothesis can be formulated to the effect that social bonds in Academia are relatively stable and, while they include bonds of 'solidarity', 'isolation' and 'engulfment', 'isolation' appears to be a dominant form.

Chapter 9
Emotional Micropolitics and Gender

Scheff's theory was employed in the previous chapter in order to elucidate the character of communication and social bonds between colleagues. A different theory developed by Candace Clark is introduced in this chapter. It concerns the ongoing discernment of social place, relative to others, within the microhierarchies of everyday life.

Academia has meritocratic traits that are expressed in competition and the struggle for position in a number of different contexts. Clark's theory considers how handling of emotions can be used as a positioning tool in everyday interactions. That is to say, it is a theory of emotional micropolitics. I have identified a number of ways in which feelings are handled in academic life, including 'the deceiving game', 'ventriloquism', anger management and the use of humour. These strategies will now be re-assessed in the light of Clark's theory of emotional micropolitics. The deceiving game, ventriloquism and so on are strategies that are commonly acknowledged by actors within the academic culture of emotions. This does not necessarily mean, however, that they are available to everyone, insofar as the actual availability of micropolitical strategies in everyday life is determined by both social position and gender.

The focus of this chapter is upon the interplay between emotional micropolitics and gender and thereby upon processes that serve to reproduce hierarchies and gender inequalities in Academia.[1] Since this meta-analysis builds upon analyses presented in earlier chapters, once again some of the excerpts we have seen earlier will be taken up for re-analysis. Candace Clark's theory of emotional micropolitics is briefly introduced in the following section.

Theory

Clark (1990, 1997, 2004) takes the concept of *social place* as her point of departure. This concept of a 'sense of place' is drawn from the work of Goffman (1951). It refers to the situated discernment of where one stands at any given moment with regard to relative power, social status and/or social distance in face-to-face interactions with others. In this light, her point is that the sense of social place, which is one aspect of the situated self, is made subjectively accessible to us by means of felt emotions, such as feelings of shame, uncertainty, fear, pleasure and so on. Social place thus refers to this sense of place on a subjective level, while on the objective

---

1 An earlier version of this analysis is published in Bloch (2003).

level it refers to differentiations of recognition and privilege. Persons who enjoy a high social place, as compared to those of low social place, have more and different interactional rights, including the right to pass judgement, have opinions listened to, arrive late, ignore others, etc. It can be said that the concept of 'social place' in micro level interactions corresponds to the concept of 'status position' in social structure on the macro level. The difference is that while status positions are stable features of social structure, subject to widespread consensus, social place is always a less clearly defined, transient and situation-dependent feature of interaction on the micro level.[2] Accordingly, far more uncertainty is usually at play in regard to the discernment of social place. While we are made aware of our status position by means of the rights and obligations accorded to us in a relatively constant manner, information about our social place is transmitted to us first and foremost by feelings such as those of uncertainty, fear, contempt, awe or admiration, which arise in the course of concrete interactions in everyday life.

Social place is always a matter of on-going negotiation, which is why Clark introduces the concept of 'micropolitics' to refer to the social practices whereby we solicit or barter our way to social place, but also practices by which we give social place to others. Since our feelings inform us about our social place in the microhierarchies of everyday life, the ways in which we handle our own feelings and those of others are important tools in the negotiation of social place.[3] Emotional micropolitics can take the form of spontaneous or strategic handling of emotions in negotiations of social place. Micropolitics can be directed towards providing social place for others or usurping it for oneself and a distinction is therefore made between two general strategies: the *Me First strategy* and the *You First strategy*. Each of these emotional micropolitical strategies includes many different ways of handling and using feelings during negotiations of social place.

It is characteristic of the 'Me First' strategy that we use feelings to solicit or lay claim to social place in interaction with others. We might, for example, try to gain social place by radiating confidence and superiority or by expressing anger, irritation or impatience with the other. We might try to confuse others by making fun of them or using some other means of making them feel uncertain of themselves. We might also seek to gain place by flattering superiors or by displaying a 'positive' feeling, such as patience, accomplished in a manner that serves to underline our own superiority and forbearance as well as the relative inferiority of the other. The

---

2   Social status affects our social place, yet the relationship is imperfect. There is not a causal relationship between status and place (Clark 1990: 300). Persons with the same social status can have different place, and persons with low social status, such as a temporarily-hired teacher with a special charisma, can gain a high social place.

3   A distinction is drawn between emotions as 'place markers' and emotions as 'place claimers'. Emotions as place markers are positive or negative self-feelings that indicate our social place. Emotions as place claimers are emotions directed at others, by means of which we indicate our superior position, for example by displaying anger towards others (Clark 1990: 310-316).

'Me First' strategy is based on the underlying assumption that the relationship is competitive and, given the character of reciprocally competitive relationships, the consideration of how the other person can be used to strengthen one's own social place is central to this strategy. In contrast, the 'You First' strategy is directed towards providing place for the other either by downplaying one's own place or by elevating the place accorded to the other, and sometimes by pursuing both policies at once. This might be done, for example by expressing positive feelings, such as praise and respect, or by avoiding practices that might confuse or bewilder the other. The underlying assumption of this strategy is that the relationship is one of cooperation, based on team spirit between equals, such that what is good for the other also serves the common good.

'Me First' and 'You First' strategies are general categories, each of which covers a range of different ways in which we claim social place, give ground to the place of others, and encounter claims for place on the part of others. Such strategies may well be effective, but they may also be rejected or interpreted in unintended ways, giving rise to further negotiations of relative social place. For example, one's aggressive comments on a colleague's research project might provoke feelings of discomfort, uncertainty and withdrawal, but might also provoke anger and counterattack.

Power and status in Academia formally speaking concern the possession of objective merits. Micropolitics, in contrast, concern a universe of tacit communication beneath the surface of situated interaction in which social place is negotiated by means of small, often unnoticed markers and cues. These negotiations take place within both hierarchical and horizontal social relations.

Clark's theory is a theory of social relationships focussed upon the interplay between the handling of emotions and the negotiation of social place. However, prevailing feeling rules also determine ways in which we handle the emotions that arise in social interactions. For example, a display of anger might prove to be an inappropriate micropolitical strategy in a context in which anger is conceived as a breach of emotional etiquette. Furthermore, different studies (Shields 2002, Pierce 1995) indicate that ways in which emotions are handled are related to prevailing conceptions of femininity and masculinity. Feeling rules are gendered, just as particular modes of expressing feeling are differently assessed, depending on whether the actor is a man or a woman. That is to say, both context and gender determine which handling strategies are experienced as being available and appropriate in a given situation.

Since gendered feeling rules arise from conceptions of gender, my analysis draws on theories of gender developed by Søndergaard and Haavind, as well as Bourdieu.[4] A pivotal point in gender theory and research in recent years (Søndergaard 1994; 1996 and Haavind 1998) is that femininity and masculinity should not be conceived in the essentialist manner as constituting a fixed dichotomy, but rather as

---

4   Bourdieu's theory of gender is presented in Bourdieu (1998). For a presentation of this theory in relation to Academia, see Bloch (1999).

a constructed distinction, the content of which is open to negotiation. Accordingly, this research distinguishes between, on the one hand, actors characterised by feminine or masculine body signs and, on the other hand, gender as a culturally constructed distinction that functions as a guiding principle of orientation with regard to interpretations and practices, both on the individual level and within the prevailing culture. Søndergaard and Haavind, but also Bourdieu (1998), emphasise the fluid and diverse character of culturally constructed distinctions regarding gender. Bourdieu (1998) describes how symbolic gender distinctions have become detached from biological characteristics and dispersed in the form of homologous distinctions that imperceptibly affect our discernments in many contexts, while Søndergaard highlights cultural differences regarding gendered codes in different contexts. The content of such codes, as already indicated, is negotiable, although there are limits to this process.[5] Both Søndergaard and Haavind also emphasise that women and men can combine expressions of masculinity and femininity from different codes in their own constructions of identity.

Recent gender research thus underlines the context-dependent character of cultural codes, the fact that codes are negotiable and that both women and men can combine modes of expression that connote femininity and masculinity, respectively. On this theoretical basis one can expect that gendered significance is ascribed to particular ways of handling emotions, and that these strategies are assessed differently depending on whether the actors involved are women or men. However, it can also be expected that at least some gendered ways of handling emotions are open to negotiation, just as – within limits – women can employ strategies that connote masculinity and men can employ strategies that connote femininity.

The four groups of emotions (shame/doubt, pride/joy, anger and laughter) and ways in which they are handled will now be discussed in the light of Clark's theory regarding the two general forms of micropolitical strategy. The focus is upon the ways in which women and men handle these emotions and on the interplay between these handling strategies, cultural codes regarding gender and social place.

Shame, Fear and Doubt

Research as an activity not only gives rise to feelings of uncertainty and doubt, but also to fear of criticism from colleagues. All interviewees were familiar with fear and doubt, and all were aware that the 'correct' way to handle these feelings was by means of practices that I have termed 'the deceiving game'. This game is

---

5   Limits to this negotiation are seen by Bourdieu (1998) as concerning the hierarchical relation between the feminine and the masculine, while Søndergaard sees them as being constituted by what she terms the 'metacode'. However, since my empirical material does not provide a basis for qualified analysis or determination of such limits as set by a metacode, no further consideration of these limits is presented here.

performed by hiding one's doubt and uncertainty behind a suitably academic facade of perspicacity, control and authority as regards one's research. The deceiving game is about not exposing oneself and not displaying weakness. However, this game is not only concerned with handling feelings on an individual level. The deceiving game is also a relational initiative, which is presented in interactions with others, and can be interpreted as constituting a 'Me First' strategy. We hide our uncertainty, our doubt and our fiascos and display instead self-confidence, superiority and authority to others. This entails the attempt to maintain or strengthen our social place within competitive relationships.

The deceiving game, it might be thought, appears to be a gender-neutral game. Yet, it is not as the following excerpts serve to illustrate. Moreover, the deceiving game is not the only strategy for handling doubt and uncertainty. Two assistant professors, the first of whom is a man and the second a woman, describe the ways in which they handle fiascos:

> Yes, well, one can share frustrations about teaching. Typically, that won't be frustration about one's own ability to cope with teaching. It would be more along the lines of being frustrated about the fact that the students are they way they are. You can always get an ear for that point of view, because every teacher knows what it's like to have students that are lethargic and haven't done their preparation. So that's often the story one tells. Not that it is anything new, but it's an invitation to respond with a "Yes, that's the way it is sometimes." And then the feeling is about sharing something or having had the same frustrations. But academic frustrations in general – I don't think I'd let my colleagues in on those. I mean, saying that this is a bit of a dead end and I've been sitting here working on something that isn't going anywhere. No, that's something I would keep to myself.

This assistant professor employs a 'Me First' strategy in relation to his abilities, both as a teacher and as a researcher. Academic frustrations are kept to himself, thereby protecting his social place in relation to potential competitors, his colleagues. He can, however, talk openly with his colleagues about his annoyance with lazy students who have not done their homework. The following response to the same question, regarding whether or not one can be open with one's colleagues about fiascos, is somewhat different:

> It is OK to talk about limited fiascos... That means for instance that if one has spent a month trying to run something or other down [in the library] and what one thought was to be found simply was not there at all, then one has wasted all that time and is on the point of going around the bend. I can talk about that kind of thing. "Do you know what?" "Now I've bloody well done it again." "That's not good at all." "What on earth will I do?" But deep, genuine doubt about my own worth – which always turns up at some point in the middle of a fruitful research process – I wouldn't dream of revealing that. They might just believe

it. I'm a woman – I look wrong. Oh, everything about me is wrong in this milieu. And that means they are all too willing to believe it, if I say there's something I can't figure out – then [they will think] there probably isn't much of anything that I can figure out at all. So I don't give them any chance to start thinking along those lines. This is a workplace for men and you don't show your weaknesses in here. So I don't show any weakness either.

This assistant professor also refrains from sharing deep existential doubt about her academic abilities with her colleagues. On that point, she plays the deceiving game. Yet, while the man behind the foregoing excerpt presents the deceiving game as a taken for granted strategy, this young woman justifies her use of this strategy by the fact that her workplace is 'a workplace for men', in which the deceiving game is the norm. Failure to play this game is interpreted as a display of 'weakness', and when women display 'weakness' they are likely to activate the idea that women cannot do research. According to this assistant professor, if she admits there is something she can't figure out, her colleagues will then think there probably isn't much of anything she can figure out at all. She believes therefore that it is particularly necessary and important for women in Academia to observe limits within which doubt and uncertainty should be kept hidden.

Both women and men employ the deceiving game. However, among the PhD fellows, some of the younger women had tried out alternatives to this strategy. It transpires from their narratives that they feel uncomfortable about the practice of deception and find it strange. In some cases they describe situations in which they had deliberately decided to reveal doubt and uncertainty. The following excerpt illustrates how a 'You First' strategy of this kind was received. This young woman had openly presented her material, her questions and her uncertainties at a PhD seminar. She had seen this seminar as an opportunity to work together with others and describes herself as having been open to and interested in hearing their opinions about her research project. In other words, she had followed a 'You First' strategy based on the assumption that cooperation was at issue. She discovers, however, that this is:

… read as a weakness. One has to manifest strength, and I didn't. Because I … well, my way of doing things is a deliberately "weak" way. I always try to just listen, and wonder, and expose myself as "weak" – because I often think that I get to know people better that way. This is just the way I do things. So, the behaviour that's normal for me is precisely to reveal the way I am and to be weak and open. This is definitely a women's thing. And it's just completely misunderstood in here. I should never have done it.

In her narrative, she oscillates between her own interpretation and her perception of her colleagues' interpretation of her way of handling doubt and uncertainty. She describes her usual approach as being deliberate, as an appropriate and fruitful way to interact with others. Yet she is also made aware that within her colleagues' frame of reference this approach is seen as an expression of weakness and an absence of strength. She classifies her own approach as being feminine in a positive sense, but also makes it clear that in the eyes of her colleagues femininity is equated with academic weakness. That is to say, she attempts to transform the homologous relationship between femininity and weakness into a homologous relationship between femininity and openness. It transpires from the rest of her narrative, however, that her colleagues merely repeat and confirm their own perception of her as being an academically confused young woman. They gain social place, while she loses social place: 'They all read me into their own things without trying to find out where I stood'. And during the pause, she is exposed to comforting remarks:

> Another "he" came over, patted me on the cheek and said that he would explain what it was all about at a later time. He suggested that we should arrange a time when I could interview him. Then he would explain to me how I could revise my theoretical perspective along the lines of his approach.

The response to her open strategy is a series of 'Me First' moves on the part of her colleagues. They do not consider the situation from her perspective and do not address her research project as such. Instead, according to this PhD fellow, they present their own academic hobbyhorses and, by displaying consolation and sympathy, they contribute further to her feelings of inferiority, which entails her loss of social place. It is first and foremost young women among the PhD fellows who describe attempts of this kind and who have tried out alternatives to the deceiving game. However, several also make it clear that they have learned from experience, and are now considering learning and actively employing the deceiving game.

Opposition to the deceiving game is also expressed by women at the other end of the academic hierarchy among associate and full professors. Some of these women had actively sought to develop a counterculture by seeking to promote collective openness with regard to doubts, uncertainties and fiascos. One assistant professor describes such an attempt on the part of her professor, who is also a woman, to develop a culture of openness with regard to research fiascos:

> We try. We've actually taken it up at a few meetings. Research fiascos are something we want to work on – because in our field we haven't been very good at talking about them. But I do think we're beginning to get to grips with it. I've tried describing some of my own fiascos – my back-of-the-drawer projects – and this works incredibly well, because everyone has fiascos (laughs)!

This attempt implies a 'You First' strategy based on cooperative relationships, the objective of which is to legitimate feelings of doubt and uncertainty by means of collective acknowledgement of the fact that we all suffer failures and run into fiascos. The person who is willing to present a 'back-of-the-drawer' project provides social place for colleagues, who together can try to help each other forward with projects that have reached a deadlock. An associate professor, also a woman, has this to say:

> I don't think everyone is [open about successes and failures]. And not everyone wants to send equally clear signals. But there are a few of us now that come out with it and tell others when we've had something published. And in the same way, when we're disappointed, we bloody well come out with that too and tell about it. My impression is that a lot of people here don't tell anyone when they've had something rejected. We don't use each other as colleagues. They're too shy or too ambitious in some way or other. I don't have any inhibitions on that score, I have to admit.

Yet openness can have its limitations, and position in the hierarchy may also be a factor in deciding where those limits lie. For example, a woman professor says:

> Ah yes, well, I have no problem talking about those [fiascos]. On the contrary, I do it actually to sort of show that not everything I do is a success – I also get conference papers rejected and that sort of thing. However, I don't think I would tell about some situation or other in which I had made a fool of my self during a meeting or something like that. That isn't exactly the kind of thing I would tell everyone, because feeling ashamed is such a very personal feeling. I think I should sort that kind of thing out for myself.

To sum up the analysis thus far, there are different ways of handling the doubts and uncertainties that arise in the course of doing research. Both women and men present the deceiving game as the acknowledged strategy for handling these feelings in Academia. This is a 'Me First' strategy, and it presents itself as a gender-neutral one. Deviations from this strategy tend to be perceived as signs of weakness, however, as when such weakness is displayed by a woman and serves to activate notions of academic weakness and femininity. The deceiving game is not explicitly linked to notions of masculinity, but its antithesis – a display of weakness – is linked to femininity, thereby indirectly suggesting that the deceiving game does indeed carry connotations of masculinity. This is not to say that women do not employ the deceiving game. Yet, as compared with men, women express more ambivalent and reflective attitudes towards the performance of this game. It is also women who contest the deceiving game by openly expressing doubts and uncertainties (employing a 'You First' strategy). This analysis indicates that such attempts to negotiate alternatives to the deceiving game within the competitive relationships of Academia are either seen as expressions of academic weakness on the part of women, leading to loss of social place, or survive as small counter-cultural islands within the larger universe of Academia.

Pride

Collegial recognition is the reward of research and, as noted earlier, pride is the feeling recognition brings. Almost all interviewees describe feelings of pride or pleasure in connection with diverse experiences of academic success. Pride is forbidden in Academia, however. Displaying one's pride is interpreted as boastful behaviour, which is conceived a being inappropriate for academics. This prohibition can be circumvented by means of 'ventriloquism', according to which pride is displayed under cover of telling an entertaining story or divulging useful information.

Both women and men experience pride in relation to their achievement of academic merit, and all are familiar with the strategy of ventriloquism. Ventriloquism can be seen as constituting a 'Me First' strategy. The ventriloquist draws attention to his or her success, thereby claiming social place relative to others (competitors). But both pride and ventriloquism are ambiguous entities. Pride can be an expression of self-esteem and delight, but also of arrogance and conceit. Ventriloquism can be conceived as a form of gift-giving between colleagues, but a given performance might be interpreted as self-promotion.

Women are not expected to express positive self-feelings such as pride. Neither are men, but in contrast to men, women accede to this prohibition (cf. Stoppard and Gruchy 1993). The general tendency to emerge from the present study confirms that men follow this pattern. They readily circumvent the prohibition on displays of pride by practising ventriloquism, a strategy which they tend to take for granted. Women, in contrast, present several different ways of handling pride. Some subscribe to a strategic, but moderated form of ventriloquism. Others subscribe to the prevailing feeling rules and adhere to this prohibition by keeping their pride well hidden. Finally, there are women who describe alternative strategies to ventriloquism. These different ways of handling pride will now be illustrated.

> I'm very careful about letting people know when I've done something outside the department ... you don't have to announce everything. I never say when I've had an article in a journal, or held something for my own professional colleagues. They know about those, of course. ... One describes a funny episode that happened at this or that conference, from which it emerges that I was present and that I was one of the keynote speakers.

This young woman employs ventriloquism, but she does so with a precise, strategic awareness of its purpose and limits. She emphasises that ventriloquism is to be used only in regard to particular kinds of events, and she underlines the behaviour of men in her department as a negative point of contrast, about whom she says:

> Colleagues that are blatant boasters, and always saying what they did and why, are really embarrassing. I'm talking about men here, since they're mostly the

ones that do that. People are so sick of them. ... There are a few who do it to such an extent that one finds them rather creepy. I'm not the only one that thinks so, that's just the way it is.

This except illustrates the ambiguous character of ventriloquism. 'Creepy' men cross the line, as she sees it, and fail to observe the limits for the appropriate use of ventriloquism. She therefore rejects their claim to social place. Other women, however, do not draw this line. Their strategy is to handle pride by keeping it entirely to themselves. They observe the prohibition on pride by maintaining silence about their success. This way of handling pride constitutes neither a 'Me First' nor a 'You First' strategy. However, its unintended consequence is that such women are rendered relatively invisible, as compared to ventriloquists, which entails that this strategy facilitates loss of social place. This may be one reason why acceptance of the prohibition on displaying pride is often shrouded in ambivalence. An associate professor, who only displays her success through the formal channel, the departmental annual report, expresses her ambivalence in the following way:

> No, we don't have any "hurray" encounters! Maybe we should too, but we don't. Well, there are limits to how much time one has to go around advertising oneself. Maybe I don't do that enough, but, well ...

She is scornful about the idea of 'advertising oneself', but also admits that she may not do it enough. A younger woman indicates a similar feeling of ambivalence more indirectly:

> I: When you experience success like that at a conference, do you tell anyone in here about it?
>
> IP: Well, previously, I didn't do that much, because I didn't think it was relevant. But now I do. I really intend to do so now.

She had earlier observed the prohibition against displaying pride and merits, but finds that this practice makes her invisible as compared to her colleagues – who, unlike her, make their successes known. But why is it first and foremost women, who express reservations about displaying pride? The following excerpts from women's narratives indicate why. An associate professor says:

> I feel sometimes that you run into – if you've had an article published in some good journal or other – you get a hint of envy. And you have the feeling that your delight is maybe not shared. It might be in an indirect way. If you have published and publish quite a lot, it might be a case of ... re-analysing some data. I link up registered sets of existing data, while there are others who sit and send out their own questionnaires. So, it's a matter of: yes, well it's okay for me just

sitting there analysing because I'm not sending out my own questionnaires and maybe I don't have that much teaching to do either. What I mean is, they keep trying to find reasons why this should be downgraded, instead of seeing it as a contribution. Sometimes one gets the sense that there is gossip going on in the corners that one isn't in on and there are times when I think that when one has had something published, there's a silence louder than words.

Another woman describes why she refrains from announcing her successes:

> Because the culture of "not blowing your own trumpet" just doesn't allow it. So, I don't do it. I think I've already got the image of being one of those our Head of department calls "the high-flyer-careerist-types". So I don't want to make matters worse than they are, because I really wouldn't like to be the kind that puts a damper on [the] motivation [of others].

Both women and men experience the envy of colleagues in Academia. The question is whether successful women are assessed differently than successful men. The aforementioned women were both highly qualified. The first speaks of her work as being downgraded and her achievements met with heavy silence, while the second supposes that she is somewhat derogatively categorised by others as a deviant 'careerist type'. The significance of gender is not explicated in these excerpts. Another associate professor does so, however, when she says:

> You've no idea how tough it is to be a successful woman in Academia. You're not only seen as a deviant, but you're also considered to be arrogant, as though you think you are worth more than others.

This view suggests that the display of positive self-feelings by women and their use of ventriloquism as a strategy for communicating success both conflict with the cultural code of gender in Academia. Women who are academically successful feel that they are treated with suspicion, such that their success and feelings of pride are best kept hidden. To the extent they pursue this strategy, however, they are rendered invisible as compared to ventriloquists and risk losing social place.

Just as it is women in Academia who try to develop alternative strategies with reference to the deceiving game, so it is also women who describe attempts to develop alternatives to ventriloquism. Once again, it is those at the associate and full professor level who describe efforts to develop an alternative culture – in this case, one that would permit the expression of pride. An associate professor says:

> There are quite a few of us that do it now [talk about being proud and delighted]. When we get something published we come out and tell everyone.

An assistant professor tells the following about her professor, who is also a woman:

> I think that our professor tries to promote a sense of pride in the department. The way she looks at it, we should actually be proud of the work we do. She tries to get the enjoyment it gives us up on a higher level, and I think that's incredibly good. She's good at handing out credit for different things we do. And that gives one – well, it feels like people are able to take more pride in the things they do.

In the following excerpt, a professor describes her feelings and thoughts about a culture that would permit open expressions of pride and her sense that others resist this possibility:

> I feel proud very rarely – either on my own behalf, personally, or on behalf of the department. I don't think we have that culture [which permits it]. I'm not sure whether this is due to our department, as such, or whether it's a question of Danish mentality. But we don't really have a culture in which you are allowed to show off any achievement – even if you do it very, very cautiously. I miss getting some kind of pat on the back and being able to see that others are just as delighted about something as one is oneself – when being pleased about each other's success would be part of building up a culture of team spirit.

This professor yearns for 'You First' relationships based on team spirit and cooperation as an alternative to competitive relationships, and in which the individual's success would be perceived as a contribution to the success of the group as a whole.

To summarise, both women and men present ventriloquism as being the acknowledged strategy for displaying the feeling of pride, but they differ in regard to their perception of the limits of this strategy. Appropriate use of ventriloquism can work as a 'Me First' strategy, but its success depends on where one draws the line. Some women perceive men as tending to far exceed the appropriate boundaries. Some women are also convinced that these boundaries are narrower for women than for men. Being academically successful and being a woman presents itself as a suspicious cocktail in Academia, insofar as it challenges the cultural code regarding gender. For this reason, women in Academia are obliged to observe the prohibition against displays of pride to a greater extent than men, while men are enabled to circumvent this prohibition in a legitimate fashion by means of ventriloquism. To the extent that men master the art of ventriloquism, their reward is greater visibility, stronger self-esteem and higher social place. Women at associate and full professor levels particularly underline the fact that the appropriate use of ventriloquism is a difficult art for women to practice. Younger women, however, express a willingness to learn and to practice ventriloquism, that is to say, to cross the boundary established by the traditional gender code. A culture open to the display of pride can be seen as a counter-cultural response to a culture in which displays of pride and academic success on the one hand and of femininity on the other, are seen as being incompatible. A counter-culture of this kind is only described by women.

Anger

Academia is an organisation that generates strong feelings of shame, bitterness and anger. The display of anger, however, is a breach of the feeling rules of Academia. As one interviewee remarks, 'It's a bit too primitive for us.' Nevertheless, everyone interviewed in the course of this study, both women and men, report episodes of felt shame and anger in relation to the struggle for recognition, resources or tenure, and describe feelings of anger that arise in response to unfair or offensive treatment. Yet, they present these feelings and their ways of handling them, in different ways. The following excerpts are examples of men's descriptions of anger in Academia. An assistant professor describes a situation in which a suggestion to break with the hitherto accepted principle of continuity regarding assistant and associate professorships was under consideration by his Faculty.[6] This had personal consequences for him, and he describes himself as having been very angry, adding, 'This led a few people, including myself, to write to [a higher authority, complaining].' Another assistant professor describes his response to delay regarding the advertisement of vacant positions in his department:

> I was very, very, very angry and I made that clear at several staff meetings. Yeah, it wasn't just me – several other jobs had been delayed. It wasn't just the notice for my job. It was the ads in general.

These assistant professors recount the anger they feel about unfair treatment, but they also describe how they express this anger either verbally or in writing. These ways of handling anger can be interpreted as constituting a 'Me First' strategy. The perception of a conflict of interests is the point of departure for angry feelings, which are then expressed as a threat, complaint or other demonstration of power in relation to others. This offensive form of anger is found in several of the narratives in which men describe negotiations undertaken in the form of face-to-face confrontation, letters of complaint or threatening e-mails. Sending angry or threatening e-mails is also characterised as being a man's way of communicating anger. An example of this kind of anger and response in a less formal situation is offered by this associate professor in his description of an episode that had taken place when he was an assistant professor:

> [I] got this really hefty reprimand in writing because I was meant to be responsible [for booking a room]. I thought it was unfair that it was me who got this telling off. So, I was fairly mad. I remember that I went in and had a real showdown with the Head of department about that. The situation really made me lose my temper. I went in and said I found it utterly unreasonable and I

---

6 This principle of 'continuity' refers to the policy whereby an appointment as assistant professor is always followed by the advertisement of an associate professorship, for which the assistant professor may apply.

demanded an apology there and then. He said he wouldn't do that. So, there was a bit of a cold atmosphere for a few weeks. Then things got back to normal again because we both gave a bit of ground.

He presents his anger as having been justified, and he indicates that he did not lose social place by handling it as he did since, as he points out, normal relations were soon resumed. It also emerges from a later part of this interview that the colleague at issue in this episode had since become an ally of the interviewee. A display of anger can command respect and accordingly contribute to gaining social place.

Like the men, women describe their anger at what they see as being unfair or unreasonable treatment. Some describe how they express that anger in formal contexts, while others first and foremost express the need to restrain any display of anger. The following illustrates the latter approach to handling this feeling. An assistant professor who has received a negative assessment from an evaluation committee feels that she has been treated very unfairly and incorrectly. She feels extremely angry about this and describes her response:

Yes, one suppresses it [the anger] in the sense that you mustn't say too much, because then you would be revealing too much about yourself.

The excerpt indicates that she considers it dangerous to reveal her anger to her colleagues. As she says, it is important not to 'say too much' about her anger and its target to her colleagues. This may be for the reason that her colleagues are likely to be her assessors again at a later date, but apart from that consideration, this assistant professor also indicates her belief that the expression of anger would be revealing in a dangerous way. Yet, it does not always prove possible to keep anger under control, which can subsequently give rise to self-reproach and feelings of uneasiness. On this point, an associate professor says:

Sometimes you can feel such a complete idiot because you're just not able to [control anger and simply agree with the Head of department]. I admire those who are able to take ownership of something [tasks, functions] – and they almost give the impression that they've accomplished something, which they haven't done at all.

She feels that a display of anger is an inappropriate path to take, but without explicating reasons why this is so. However, the following excerpts serve to illustrate the way in which women in Academia perceive the reception of a display of anger on their part. A professor recounts how she feels angry about what she feels is misuse of her time:

I can remember some other situations, although I no longer remember why they arose, but there were some situations in which I got angry, irritated and impatient at some departmental meetings. Some of my colleagues were deeply shocked that this hard woman [herself] could express feelings. But when I do erupt in that kind of way, I think most of my colleagues just think to themselves that there must be something I can't cope with or handle. So they react to it in a kind of evasive way. At any rate, I've been told several times – by my Head of department, at least – that I simply must express myself in a cooler fashion.

This woman does not always keep her anger under control. Her colleagues' reaction is to label her as a person who cannot cope with the given situation, and to otherwise react evasively to such outbursts, while her Head of department has suggested how she should behave instead. That is to say, displays of anger on her part entail a loss of social place. It also emerges from men's narratives that angry women are perceived as being 'hysterical', 'quick-tempered' or 'cantankerous'. One man, an associate professor, expresses the view this way:

> It's mainly the women who get angry. We have a few of them – one is, well, cantankerous (laughs), and the other is a real sourpuss. That's when she feels she's being treated unfairly – and then it [an angry outburst] is in front of others!

Angry women in Academia tend to be interpreted by men as having lost control, as being weak and powerless, or as lacking femininity. This entails that women risk losing social place when they are perceived as being angry, such that there is good reason why women should try to control their anger. Self-control and suppression of anger are not without cost, however. The suppression of shame and anger can give rise to social withdrawal. For the most part, it is women who present examples of helpless anger followed by withdrawal and alienation from others, while it is men who present examples of explosive anger. Explosive anger constitutes a breach of the prevailing feeling rules, but it does not contribute to social invisibility.

Summarising these results, it can be said that, in principle, anger is a proscribed emotion in Academia, but it is nonetheless an emotion that is familiar to everyone. Women, according to Shields (2002), focus more on loss of control in regard to their anger, while men focus on the justification of their anger. This pattern is also apparent in the present study. Men in Academia tend to describe their anger as a show of strength, while women describe the need to keep their anger under control. These strategies with regard to handling anger are supported by interpretations of displays of anger on the part of women and men, respectively. Angry women are seen as being weak and powerless, as ill-tempered or hysterical, while anger in men tends to be presented and interpreted as a show of strength. This interplay between anger, strength and gender is expressed in the following way by a woman PhD fellow:

> They [men, older colleagues] did not attack me head on, as they would have done with a man PhD fellow, so I just let my head turn from one to the other. If I'd become angry, I think they might have shown me more respect.

This excerpt indicates the complex interplay between anger and gender in Academia. Anger is also employed in stand-off battles and academic disputes between men. Women and their academic standing are not drawn into battles of this kind. They are not exposed to the explosive anger of academic dispute, and they are not expected to display anger. Rather, they tend to be overlooked, deemed invisible and, in the manner described by this PhD fellow, treated as a spectator – even when their own research project is under discussion. This young woman wonders whether she could have gained more respect by showing her anger. The question is, however, whether this would have helped her. A display of anger on her part might well have been interpreted as an expression of powerlessness and weakness. This compels women to try to keep angry feelings under control, but anger is not something we can easily control. It can be transformed into other feelings and it can give rise to social withdrawal, the unintended effect of which is invisibility, that is to say, loss of social place. The patterns that emerge from this analysis indicate that no matter which strategies women in Academia choose with regard to handling anger, they tend to lose social place, whereas men can gain social place by their display of anger.

Laughter

Laughter and humour have previously been described as liberating ways of handling conflict and tension. Insofar as humour serves to relieve tension by means of shared feelings of amusement, it can be interpreted as constituting a 'You First' strategy. Humour is a valued competence in Academia and accordingly serves to gain social place. However, the precondition of shared amusement is that people do interact to an extent that allows them to construct a shared social reality, which then can become the object of humour. Although colleagues in Academia do not meet each other to any notable extent, it was possible to identify 'ground floor humour' and 'joking relationships' as informal communities in which a sense of humour is shared. A PhD fellow says for example:

> Yeah, well I'd say we have a good laugh every day in the laboratory. It happens a lot. Well, actually, it happens every day. Jokes are cracked all the time, so there's a lot of grinning and a good deal of hilarity. We have a number of smaller laboratories and some of the lads are in one of them and we sit cracking bawdy jokes all day long (laughs). Not because we're all (laughs) that bad…(laughs)

This man indicates that some communities of bawdy jokes are exclusive to 'the lads', but it is by no means only men among the PhD fellows who laugh together and tell each other jokes. As one of the women remarks:

> We do that a lot [laugh] in the lunch pause, and when we're sitting around running tests. I think we're very, very good at it.

She continues:

> We laugh about private things and academic stuff, or just a funny remark, a joke – we're experts at telling dirty jokes at the lunch table. It can be all kinds of things. And it's not all just a long laugh. I actually think we're good at sitting and chatting about more serious things too. It's simply that we're all good friends in one way or the other.

Among PhD fellows, both men and women describe situations in which they share 'dirty jokes' and laugh a lot together in both mixed and mono-gendered groups. Some of the men recount that jokes are a bit different when women are present. However, women and men at this level experience a shared social reality, which serves as the basis for shared humour that takes its point of departure in their common position at the bottom of the academic hierarchy. One pokes fun at academic norms and at the professor, makes bawdy remarks and tells each other dirty jokes. It is quite apparent that this form of humour contributes to a sense of community among PhD fellows, and can be interpreted as constituting a 'You First' strategy.

This picture changes as we move up the academic hierarchy. Becoming an assistant or associate professor entails an individualisation and specialisation and the character of social relationships changes accordingly. As described in Chapter 6, a particular form of humorous interaction develops, that I have termed 'joking relationships'. One man describes this form in the following way:

> Yes, yes, and then we twist things that have been said! There are a couple of people who are really good at that. We often tease and kid each other a bit during coffee breaks, you know?

Joking relationships unfold over lunch, during coffee breaks and in corridors and offices. They are characterised by teasing, making ironic, politically incorrect or provocative remarks and similar forms of banter. Joking relationships can be interpreted as constituting a 'You First' strategy that promotes feelings of togetherness in a positive way, but they also have a competitive character, which is consistent with a 'Me First' strategy. People tease and provoke each other and, according to this excerpt, some are better at doing this than others. Furthermore, this form of humour may have a gendered content, reserved for men. As one associate professor puts this point: 'Men's jokes are more risqué, more coarse in tone [as compared to situations in which women are present].' Many narratives support the view that the form of communication practiced in joking relationships is exclusive to or generally reserved for men. This is expressed in men's remarks such as the following:

> Yes, I've only seen men do it – but it's also a sign of superiority, you know? Because it's about being in control of the situation, isn't it? And you can use the jokes for that.

> Ha, ha, ha – at any rate there are some striking gender differences in their content [humorous remarks made when women are present] (laughs). And there are definitely also gender barriers one does not cross.
>
> If fun and banter are an emotion (laughs) I think that at any rate some of the men I'm in contact with in this department find it [fun and banter] easier to express than some of the women.

And the same view emerges clearly in the following sequence:

> I: As regards that kind of teasing and kidding, is it your impression that there is any difference between the men and the women?
>
> IP: Well, yes, that – that kind of carry on is, "Men only"!
>
> I: Men only?
>
> IP: Yes.
>
> I: You say that very emphatically?
>
> IP: Yes, ah, well, ah (pause), ah, that sort of thing, making wisecracks and teasing by twisting what people say, that kind of stuff belongs on the "men only" side.

According to men, women stand outside the sphere of competitively-oriented joking relationships. However, some communities of humour among women are also described. For example, an assistant professor at the only department in this study, in which a majority of positions are held by women, describes how she and her women colleagues laugh a lot together – among other matters they enjoy parodying the male professors. A male assistant professor in a different department describes the community of humour among the women there:

> Well, I'd say that when I hear my good women colleagues – now I have to say too that I think, I mean, in precisely this department there's a relatively even mix of men and women. Not at the highest levels, but in fact so high up that it's starting to even out at the associate professor level too, and at any rate it's there among the PhD fellows and assistant professors. That must be very close to fifty-fifty – and a whole lot of them on this corridor are women who are involved in [a research initiative reserved for women applicants], so that belonging to the right gender is a prerequisite. I can hear that things are just as lively when they're together as when the men are.

Women laugh together and parody male professors. Nor is joking about gender a prerogative of men, as illustrated by an earlier excerpt:

> There was a particular group of guys [who behaved in a destructive way during teaching], so at one point, when this had been going on for a whole morning, I finally asked: "What would you call [man's name] if he were a woman?" And then one of the young women replied on behalf of the students: "We would say he was premenstrual (laughs), because he's always in such a mouldy sulk." This was her way of tackling it. I would never have dared to be so personal. The women had a great laugh altogether because, ah, well, suddenly that destructiveness, which we all felt that [man's name] and his cohorts had been displaying, was given a name.

Humour and laughter can have either an including or an excluding character. 'Ground floor' humour at the PhD level tends to include both women and men, and to maintain a basis for cooperation and solidarity. At the assistant and associate professor level, however, men describe competitively-oriented 'joking relationships' as being largely or exclusively the reserve of men. 'Joking relationships' can be characterised as constituting a 'You First' strategy between men, but a 'Me First' strategy towards women insofar as – according to men – women do not enter into these relationships. Women do not describe 'joking relationships' among themselves, but rather laughter and humour of different kinds in situations that are dominated by women or in which they constitute a majority. However, descriptions of these situations are no more than sparsely represented in my interview material, in contrast to descriptions of 'joking relationships' among men. A few women express the view that men are better at bantering and making humorous remarks. Some few also express the view that there is not much to laugh about in Academia. One woman, an associate professor, says:

> Yes, laughter, that's not something I have felt like doing in here – ever (laughs)! I have thought about it though – as something that is very characteristic [of this place]. For example, in all kinds of other contexts I have a good sense of humour and I can crack some really funny remarks. But I've never done that in here. So this place doesn't tickle my sense of humour.

To summarise, this analysis highlights a competitive, playful form of humour that exhibits both 'Me-First' and 'You First' characteristics, the practice of which contributes to gaining social place. Both the form and the content of these 'joking relationships' are reserved primarily for men. Women also describe laughter and humour, however, and it is my hypothesis that narratives concerning this humour are sparsely represented in my material for the reason that women are underrepresented in Academia and often work in settings in which men constitute a large majority. The prerequisite for humour is a shared social reality, with which one can play. Due to their limited representation and scattered locations, particularly at the higher levels of the academic hierarchy, women in Academia do not have the same social conditions as men to gain access to a community of humour and its emotional rewards. For this reason women in Academia tend to be perceived as lacking a sense of humour, which entails loss of social place.

Gender and Social Place

I have employed Clark's theory with a view to identifying some of the social microprocesses by means of which microhierarchies and gender inequalities are constructed and reproduced in Academia. These microprocesses arise from the emotions of academics and the prevailing culture of emotions. This culture favours particular strategic ways of handling emotions, the adoption of which in turn creates differences and hierarchies between people. Moreover, these strategies are not gender-neutral. Men in Academia tend to take these strategies for granted as constituting the rules of the game, whereas women tend to be much more reflective about using these strategies. At the same time, the ways of handling emotions that are available to women unintentionally entail loss of social place, that is to say, loss of visibility, recognition and interactional rights. This does not mean that all men are adept players of ventriloquism and the deceiving game or that no women employ these strategies successfully. Rather, this analysis has identified qualitatively distinct patterns that illustrate some of the processes through which men and women are assigned social place.[7]

According to Kemper's theory, felt differences in power and status generate particular emotions. Clark's theory elucidates this interplay from the opposite pole: the ways in which we handle emotions generate power and status differences within everyday interactions.

Social place in the everyday interactions of academic life and social position in the academic hierarchy are by no means the same.[8] Nonetheless, the aggregate outcome of emotional micropolitics is often the reproduction of a social order on

---

7 In Asmar's (1999) analysis of gender barriers it is noted that, despite their high level of performance, younger women researchers lack belief and confidence in themselves and in their careers. In her discussion of these barriers, she argues the need for studies of how women 'feel' their situation in Academia. My analysis identifies some of the processes that underlie the ways in which academic women 'feel' their situation.

8 There is a need for more detailed, prospective studies regarding which aspects of social place are converted to 'capital'/social position within Academia. For example, it can be thought that some people achieve respect and gain social place by virtue of personal qualities, without thereby gaining access to academic support and opportunities that help to advance academic position. There might also be people who achieve social place on the basis of real or apparent academic expertise, while the conditions for converting social place to social positions within Academia are limited by factors at other levels, such as departmental policy regarding which fields of research are prioritised. Further studies

the micro-level that contributes to the reproduction of prevailing power relations at the macro-level (Clark 1997). Social place concerns the situated negotiation of one's place in the microhierarchies of everyday life. However, social place is not merely a fluctuating phenomenon in social life. It is discerned on the basis of our emotions and can thereby obtain relative stability, become a self-reinforcing dynamic that attains the character of being taken for granted. To the extent that social place is confirmed by interaction rights conferred and recognition given, opening the way to academic support, resources and networks, it is probable that high social place is career-enhancing, while peripheral or subordinate social place will hardly be conducive to career advancement.

Clark's theory of emotional micropolitics elucidates the manner in which emotions and the ways in which they are handled constitute active forces in the ongoing reproduction of meritocratic and hierarchic structures. 'Me First' strategies can be seen as micro-level contributions to the reproduction of Academia's meritocratic structure, which is indeed based on competition and hierarchy. This analysis also contributes therefore to the identification of some of the micro-mechanisms, which contribute to shortfall regarding the recruitment of women to academic positions, as well as some of the reasons why women advance more slowly than men in the academic hierarchy (Henningsen and Højgård 2002).

---

are called for regarding the interplay between social place and academic position and its conditions.

Chapter 10
Conclusion and Perspectives

We are always emotional. Human emotionality is an ongoing stream that pervades every aspect of our social lives.

In the preceding chapters, emotional aspects of university life have been described by PhD fellows, as well as assistant, associate and full professors. They have all described concrete emotional episodes and I have identified some of the strategies they employ when handling these emotions, using concepts such as 'segmented emotion work', the 'politics of friendliness', the 'deceiving game', 'ventriloquism', 'ground floor humour' and 'joking relationships'.

Emotions are adapted to cultural norms and handled in ways that are sensitive to these norms, but they are also forces that arise from and generate relationships between people. I have tried to demonstrate the ways in which particular emotions arise from the 'specific structure' of Academia and can become transformed into non-conscious spirals of emotion that impair communication between social groups and damage collegial relationships. I have also sought to highlight the interplay between the meritocratic structure of Academia, the handling of emotions and informal hierarchies in academic life – one function of which, in conjunction with gendered feeling rules, is to support the inclusion of men and the exclusion of women.

By means of these analyses, I have drawn a tentative map of the social-emotional world of Academia. There are many different emotions in Academia. I have focussed on some of them, but there are many others. This map is therefore far from complete, since large uncharted areas have been left unexamined. Furthermore, my analyses are qualitative. I have identified some patterns, but this study does not inform us about the prevalence of those patterns. It must be emphasised therefore that my analyses have not told the full story about emotions in Academia.

As stated in the Preface, I have presented the results of this study at international research conferences and at a number of universities and institutions in Scandinavia. Some participants have pointed out that the feelings and emotional dynamics I describe are also found in other organisations. This is quite true. My objective has been to clarify the way in which particular kinds of social structure tend to generate particular kinds of emotions. However, meritocratic and hierarchic structures are not restricted to academic organisations, which is the reason why we also find envy, anger, pride and humour in other organisations, just as damaged social relationships and 'Me First' strategies are by no means restricted to the university world. Having acknowledged the truth of this, I nevertheless maintain that Academia does have features that distinguish it from other organisations.

These include its 'specific structure' and its historically-based culture of emotions, as well as the emotion of passion, which belongs to the activity of doing research.

Academia emerges from my analysis as being a somewhat unpleasant and acrimonious workplace. Yet, paradoxically, we also know that most academics do not wish to leave it. Emotional ambivalence towards their place of work on the part of academics clearly emerges from the study undertaken by Ehn and Löfgren (2004), and helps to explain this paradox. They employ the term 'mixed feelings' to summarise their findings regarding academics' feelings about university life. On the one hand, academics describe the pleasure, enthusiasm and passion they derive from their research and from fruitful cooperation with colleagues. On the other hand, they speak of the anger, disappointment, resignation, envy, sadness and depression that are also part of academic life. The title of my book is 'Passion and Paranoia'. It must be admitted, however, that my analysis has focused upon the structural and cultural basis of the darker side of academic life, in both social and emotional terms. Yet there are other strong and more uplifting emotions at work in Academia also. These positive emotions have received less attention in this study, yet it is perhaps precisely in 'mixed feelings' that the emotional tone of Academia is expressed. This may be the reason why academics remain in academic life, despite their feelings of resignation, disappointment and anger.

This is a qualitative study of emotional processes, but also one that has sought to analyse emotions as being rooted in and stabilised by the social structures and culture of a particular kind of organisation. The analytical framework derived from this theoretical approach has contributed to the robustness of its findings, but it does not elucidate the prevalence of these processes as such. For this reason, I would like to supplement my findings by considering some results from quantitative studies of Danish university departments undertaken by the Danish education researcher, Bo Jacobsen (2001a, 2001b).[1] Jacobsen does not describe his work as regarding emotions and social relationships, but rather what he terms 'departmental atmospheres'.[2] According to Jacobsen, the 'atmosphere' of a department is a social fact, in the sense that all interviewees – academics employed in a given department – can relate to this phenomenon, so described. His survey finds that 40

---

1   The sample on which this work is based comprises all academic employees at 12 university departments in Denmark (N=258), the departments being selected to maximise variability. Data were collected using a semi-structured questionnaire.

2   Jacobsen's concept of 'atmosphere' is based on the German phenomenologist Otto Friedrich Bollnow's theory of 'stimmungen' or 'moods' (Bollnow 1974; 1989). A related concept is that of 'emotional climate', which includes both a structural and phenomenological dimensions. This concept is originally associated with the work of Renato Taigura (1968), but has since been developed by Joseph de Rivera. Emotional climate is defined as the collective experience of the emotional mood in a group. This experience is based on shared structural conditions and on particular emotional relationships between the members of the group (Rivera 1992). The concept of emotional climate more easily accords with my theoretical framework, but in phenomenological terms there is little difference between the concepts of 'atmosphere' and 'emotional climate'.

per cent of academics rate the atmosphere of their department as being 'medium' or 'poor'. This figure suggests that the 'atmosphere' of their departments is viewed as being somewhat problematic by a considerable proportion of academics. But what is the significance of a problematic departmental atmosphere? Jacobsen's survey finds that 92 per cent of academics state that the departmental atmosphere at their place of work to a greater or lesser extent affects their mood and personal sense of well-being, while 62 per cent hold that the atmosphere affects their research activities (2001a). Jacobsen also investigated the correlation between the assessments of departmental atmosphere and the quality of its research output. A clear correlation was found between the assessments of 'atmosphere' on the one hand and the assessments of 'research quality' on the other as compared with similar departments in other countries. That is to say, the atmosphere or emotional climate of a university department not only affects the well-being of academic employees, but apparently also the quality of their research.[3] We might well wonder why this is the case, and precisely how departmental atmosphere does affect the quality of research. The distinction drawn by the Australian sociologist Jack Barbalet (2004, 2009) between *self-asserting* and *self-transcending* emotions helps to throw light upon this issue.

According to Barbalet, self-asserting emotions inform us about where we stand in relation to our needs, our preferences and our self-interest. They demand that external and internal stimuli be discerned and judged in terms of their relevance to the individual, and they accordingly call for a narrowing of conscious awareness such that the aspects focussed upon are instrumental or practical attributes relevant to the fulfilment of personal needs and self-interest. Emotions such as fear, shame, anger and pride are examples of self-asserting emotions. One has an article rejected, for example, and this threat to one's self-interest triggers anger. Awareness becomes focused upon the rejection. What precisely was said? What does the reviewer mean by that? Who can this reviewer be? One feels an urge to act – to tell one's colleagues, for example, or to complain to the editor. Yet, having learned from experience, one may end up deciding to try to keep one's anger in check. Self-asserting emotions usually have clear physiological correlates and are associated with specific types of behaviour.

There is also another kind of emotion, however, the intentionality of which is not directed at asserting and defending self-needs in this narrow sense. These are self-transcending emotions. These emotions are not usually consciously discerned and they accordingly tend to remain unnoticed. Moreover, while self-asserting emotions mediate a narrowing of conscious awareness, self-transcending emotions tend to widen the scope of conscious awareness by decentring awareness of self and focussing instead upon the character of the object of awareness, its structure and context. According to Barbalet, the distinction

---

3 For other studies that document the relationship between working environments and the quality of research, see Gulbrandsen (2000), Singh and Krishnaiah (1989) and Knorr, Mittermeir, Aichholzers and Waller (1979).

between self-asserting and self-transcending emotions is central to understanding the role of emotions in scientific research. He particularly emphasises the role of aesthetic feeling as a central force in the creation of new knowledge. Aesthetic feeling is a self-transcending emotion, which is disinterested in the sense that it arises from focussing exclusively on the appearance or structure of the object under scrutiny. As a consequence of disinterested concentration, instrumental or practical attributes of the object – which relate more directly to the needs of self-assertion – are placed out of focus. In this way, the intrinsic properties of objects are emotionally apprehended. Aesthetic feeling in scientific research thus entails an expansion of consciousness and an anticipation of connections, which are expressed in methodological choices and assessments of relevance. In this manner, apparent chaos can become transformed into a new order characterised by wholeness, uniqueness and aliveness. Precisely these values are, according to Maslow, integral to aesthetic experiences.[4] This transformation of chaos into new patterns is a process that brings a joyous sense of fulfilment and aesthetic pleasure. We can subsequently take pleasure in our results, but we are rarely aware of the aesthetic emotional processes that are integral to the research process itself.[5]

Barbalet's distinction paves the way for understanding the ways in which different kinds of emotions can contribute to any given process of scientific research. A highly competitive departmental atmosphere will tend to generate self-asserting emotions that support a narrow self-interest in the research process, while a departmental atmosphere characterised by solidarity is more likely to pave the way for self-transcending emotions that generate the conditions under which new insights and new knowledge can emerge. Thus, the distinction between these two kinds of emotions indicates the character of a link at the emotional level between types of departmental atmosphere and the quality of research. It should be said that the research community is partially aware of some of these emotional dynamics. Thus, the research community is aware of the disturbing influence of self-interest upon the research process. This is expressed in the norm of disinterestedness – an institutionalised demand, which is also included in Merton's CUDOS.[6] However, the research community's response to the dangers of self-interest is not only the formulation of a demand to observe the value of disinterestedness, but also a more general prohibition against emotions in Academia and in research. This entails that the research community not only remains ignorant of the significance of self-transcending emotions in the creation of new knowledge, it also ignores the fact that academic structures provide a fertile ground for the generation of self-asserting emotions.

---

4   Maslow, as cited in Kemper (1978: 303).
5   Barbalet (2011) also terms these emotions 'background emotions'.
6   Most researchers subscribe to the Mertonian set of norms regarding good scientific practice – commonly referred to by the acronym CUDOS, in which D refers to disinterestedness (Cf. Anderson 2000, Anderson, Martinson and Vries 2007).

During recent decades, the classical university has been subjected to increasing demands for 'modernisation' (Baert and Shipman 2005, Bourdieu 2005). Recurring themes of this endeavour have been the effort to streamline the university as an organisation that undertakes the education of highly-qualified manpower and contributes to the development of knowledge that can be easily converted into utilities that satisfy the needs of the business community and the wider society. These modernisation efforts are ongoing at all levels, from the level of top management all the way down to the inner mental universe of the individual academic (Krejsler 2011). New public management is the important instrument in this respect. At management level, new public management entails the replacement of academic managers by professional managers (and by managerialism). In addition, a number of different evaluation systems have been developed as tools for the quantifiable assessment of productivity. These include bibliometric indicator systems, designed to assess the productivity of research, and educational statistics designed to measure efficiency, as expressed by number of examinations held, number of graduates, number of completed PhDs, time spent completing courses of education, etc. These parameters are then employed to benchmark universities, faculties, departments and academic staff relative to each other, thereby providing a basis on which funding is allocated. Moreover, attempts to influence or control the topics of university research in a manner that accords with national interests or the interests of the business community are made by restructuring national grant systems, reducing funding for basic research, increasing the funds available for applied research and, more generally, by increasing dependence upon externally funded research. This trend supports the logic of applied research at the expense of basic research and the logic of utilitarian and commercial relevance at the expense of free research. The keywords in this process of modernisation are competition and quantity. There is nothing wrong with competition as such, although the logic of competitive output is far from well-documented (Ågård 2011). However, competition at all levels increases the competitive struggle at every level, such that the struggle for position intensifies the formation of hierarchical structures from below, while the struggle to retain privileges intensifies the importance of these structures from above (Schoug 2004). The point at issue here concerns what intensified competition entails for the emotional lives of competitors. We currently know little about this topic. Based on the preceding discussion, however, it can be thought that intensified competition generates self-asserting emotions at the expense of self- transcending emotions. That is to say, the conscious awareness of researchers is narrowed and limited by the introduction of self-interested goals, at the expense of reaching new breakthroughs in research.[7] These tendencies are taken up in debate at universities and in qualitative studies among academic staff, which highlight ways in which so-called 'modernisation' influences research.

---

7 According to Andersen et al., cooperation is positively correlated with behavior that accords with the norms of good scientific practice, while competition is positively correlated with counter norms (Anderson, Martinson and Vries 2007).

Researchers speak for example of the "salami method", according to which the results of a given research project are structured with a view producing the maximum number of articles for publication in journals with maximum exposure, and at the fastest possible rate (Wright 2009). Researchers describe how they select research topics within known areas and within the bounds of normal science, since alternative strategies would prove too time consuming and would fail to meet the demand for frequent and rapid publication. Books are rejected as a publication channel in favour of publication in journals, because the latter rate higher points (Krejsler 2011, 2007). Finally, more and more attention is being paid to the issue of scientific misconduct and to the question of what constitutes poor scientific practice (Martinson, Anderson and Vries 2005). There are no systematic records regarding the incidence of different forms of forbidden or poor scientific practices over time, but studies do show that scientific misconduct (fabrication of data, plagiarism, etc.) is particularly pronounced in research environments in which competition is most intense (Fanelli 2010). This development in the researcher's approach to his or her field of research has been characterised by Krejsler as constituting a shift from research as a project in itself to the individual researcher as a project in his/herself.

Academia has been the subject of an intense political struggle between proponents of the independent classical university on the one hand and proponents of the endeavour to streamline Academia in accordance with the needs of the business community and the wider society on the other. This book is not intended to constitute a defence of the classical university. From the perspective of the theory of emotions, its objective has rather been to highlight some of the contradictions and pitfalls inherent in the structure and culture of Academia, including its classical form. However, the analyses undertaken here also indicate that the trend towards the so-called modernisation of Academia in all probability exacerbates these, not least by tending to generate self-asserting emotions at the expense of the self-transcending emotions of research.

The purpose of this book has been to highlight the emotional dimensions of life in Academia and their significance. The analysis has sought to reveal the interplay between social structure, the prevailing culture of emotions, socio-emotional relationships and the character of scientific production, but it has not addressed all of the structural aspects that would call for consideration in any more extensive analysis and discussion of the development of Academia as a social institution. Nevertheless, this analysis of emotional processes does provide a point of departure with regard to identifying phenomena that could and should be taken into account when discussing the development and future of Academia.

The culture of Academia is one from which feelings are absent – a culture of 'no feeling'. As this book has shown, however, feelings abound in Academia. The concept of 'emotional intelligence' has recently gained the status of being a key concept in organisational theory and modern management theory. At the psychological level, emotional intelligence refers to the ability to perceive, assess and express feelings, the ability to use feelings to promote cognitive activities, the ability to understand emotion-relevant concepts and to use feeling-relevant language and, finally, the ability to handle one's own feelings and those of other persons in ways that seek to promote development, well-being and functional social relationships (Barrett and Salovey 2002). Within organisation theory, emotional intelligence concerns the ability of an organisation to acknowledge emotions as real information and to recognise their significance for the organisation's practice.

Emotional intelligence can thus be viewed as a tool for gaining insight into the emotional pitfalls inherent in the classical university, which are exacerbated by its so-called process of modernisation. It can also be a tool to deconstruct the gendered feeling rules that this analysis has identified as an active, micro-level force in the production of gender bias, which is found in most universities throughout the world today.[8] Academic culture prohibits emotions. Emotional intelligence does not prohibit emotions, but acknowledges their place, hereby questioning the character of a culture of emotions that deems them absent and challenging the feeling rules that currently prevail. Cultural changes do not take place independently of structural changes, but a given culture can take the form of questioning and challenging prevailing structures over time.

Emotions are important signals. They often have a moral aspect. They have an energy aspect, a particular inherent dynamic, and they most often occur at a non-conscious level. With the help of different groups in Academia, I have identified some of the feelings at play in academic life and have highlighted their importance for the character of social relationships in Academia. I have also sought to draw some further implications of that analysis by discussing the way in which emotions can contribute – or fail to contribute – to the *raison d'être* of Academia: the production of ground-breaking research. On this point, I have indicated some possibly unintended consequences of the prevailing structure and culture of Academia. As already stated, this analysis of emotions does not present the full story of Academia. It does indicate, however, some important dimensions that have hitherto been overlooked by the sociology of science. These can remain ignored, but they can also be integrated into our understanding and our discussion of Academia and its development, and thereby play a role in the political struggle with regard to its future.

---

8   Gender inequality in Academia at professorial level is a common and ingrained phenomenon. The following are references to studies that consider this issue in Australia (Currie, Thiele and Harris 2002), in the USA (Collins, Chrisler and Quina 1998), and in Israel (Toren 2000).

References

Aagaard, K. 2011. *Kampen om basismidlerne*. Århus Universitet: Center for forskningsanalyse.
Abu-Lughod, L. 1991. Writing Against Culture, in *Recapturing Anthropology: Working in the Present*, edited by R.G. Fox. Santa Fe: School of American Research, 137–62.
Albrow, M. 1992. Sine Ira et Studio – or Do Organizations Have Feelings? *Organization Studies*, 13(3), 313–29.
Albrow, M. 1997. *Do Organizations Have Feelings?* London: Routledge.
Anderson, M.S. 2000. Normative orientations of university faculty and doctoral students. *Science and Engineering Ethics*, 6(4), 443–61.
Anderson, M.S., Martinson, B.C. and Vries, R. 2007. Normative Dissonance in Science: Results from a National Survey of U.S. Scientists, *Journal of Empirical Research on Human Research Ethics*, 2, 1–14.
Appel, M. 2000. *Kreativ konkurrens eller hämmende hierarki. Rapport om akademins arbetsmiljö ur forskarstuderandes synvinkel*. Umeå Universitet: Centrum för folkhälsoforskning.
Appel, M. 2003. *Forskarhandledning. Möte med vandrare och medvandrare på vetenskapens vägar*. Stockholm: Högskoleverket.
Arber, A. 1954. *The Mind and the Eye: A Study of the Biologist's Standpoint*. Cambridge: Cambridge University Press.
Ashforth, B.E. and Tomiuk, M.A. 2000. Emotional Labour and Authenticity: Views from Service Agents, in *Emotion in Organizations*, 2nd Edition edited by S. Fineman. London: Sage, 184–203.
Asmar, C. 1999. Is there a gendered agenda in academia? The research experience of female and male PhD graduates in Australian universities. *Higher Education*, 38, 225–73.
Asplund, J. 1987. *Om hälsningsceremonier, mikromakt och asocial pratsomhet*. Göteborg: Bokförlaget Korpen.
Baert, P. and Shipman, A. 2005. University under Siege. *European Societies*, 7(2), 157–87.
Barbalet, J. 2002. Science and Emotions, in *Emotions and Sociology*, edited by J. Barbalet. Oxford: Blackwell Publishing, 132–51.
Barbalet, J. 2004. Consciousness, Emotions, and Science, in *Advances in-Group Processes: A Research Annual*, edited by J. Turner. Amsterdam: Elsevier Science, Vol. 21, 245–72.

Barbalet, J. 2009. Consciousness, Emotions, and Science, in *Theorizing Emotions*, edited by D. Hopkins, J. Kleres, H. Flam and H. Kuzmics. New York: Campus Verlag, 39–73.
Barbalet, J. 2011. Emotions beyond Regulation: Backgrounded Emotions in Science and Trust. *Emotion Review*, 3(1), 36–43.
Barnes, B. (ed.) 1972. *Sociology of Science*. London: Penguin Books.
Barrett, L.F. and Salovey, P. (eds), 2002. *The Wisdom in Feeling*. London: The Guilford Press.
Becher, T. and Trowler, P.R. 2001. *Academic Tribes and Territories*. Buckingham (UK) and Philadelphia (USA): SRHE and Open University Press.
Ben-Ze'ev, A. 2000. *The Subtlety of Emotions*. London: The MIT Press.
Bloch, C. 1996. Emotions and Discourse. *Text*, 16(3), 323–41.
Bloch, C. 1999. Køn i Akademia, ud fra Bourdieus blik. *Køn i den akademiske organisation*. Arbejdspapir nr. 8.
Bloch, C. 2001. *Flow og Stress. Stemninger og følelseskultur i hverdagslivet*. København: Samfundslitteratur.
Bloch, C. 2002a. Managing the emotion of competition and recognition, in *Emotions and Sociology*, edited by J. Barbalet. Oxford: Blackwell Publishing, 113–32.
Bloch, C. 2002b. Følelser og sociale bånd i Akademia. *Dansk Sociologi*, 13(4), 42–61.
Bloch, C. and Dalsgård, A.L. 2002c. Om kriterier for anerkendelse i Akademia – fra adjunktens synsvinkel. *Køn i den Akademiske Organisation*, Arbejdspapir nr. 11. København: Specialtrykkeriet Viborg a/s.
Bloch, C. 2003. Følelsernes skjulte spil i Akademia, in *Akademisk tilblivelse*, edited by L. Højgård and D.M. Søndergård. København: Akademisk forlag, 121–59.
Bollnow, O.F.V. 1974. *Das Wesen der Stimmungen*. Frankfurt: Vittorio Klostermann.
Bollnow, O.F.V. 1989. *Mensch und Raum*. Stuttgart: Verlag W. Kohlhammer.
Bourdieu, P. 1975. The specificity of the scientific field and the social conditions of the programs of reason. *Social Science Information*, 14(6), 19–47.
Bourdieu, P. 1988. *Homo Academicus*. Cambridge: Polity Press.
Bourdieu, P. 1998. *La domination masculine*. Paris: Seuil.
Bourdieu, P. 2005. *Viden om viden og refleksivitet*. København: Hans Reitzels Forlag.
Bowen, M. 1978. *Family Therapy in Clinical Practice*. New York: J. Aronson.
Bowen, M. and Kerr, M.K. 1988. *Family Evaluation*. New York: W.W. Norton & Company.
Buber, M. 1958. *I-Thou*. New York: Scribners.
Clark, C. 1990. Emotions and Micropolitics in Everyday Life: Some Patterns and Paradoxes of Place, in *Research Agendas in the Sociology of Emotions*, edited by T.D. Kemper. Albany: State University of New York Press, 303–33.
Clark, C. 1997. *Misery and Company*. London: University of Chicago Press.

Clark, C. 2004. Emotional Gifts and 'You First' Micropolitics: Niceness in the Socioemotional Economy, in *Feelings and Emotions*, edited by A.S.R. Manstead, N. Frijda and A. Fischer. Cambridge: Cambridge University Press, 402–22.
Cole, S. 1983. The hierarchy of the sciences. *American Journal of Sociology*, 89 (1), 111–39.
Collins, L.H., Chrisler, J.C. and Quina, K. 1998. *Career Strategies for Women in Academe*. Thousand Oaks: Sage.
Collins, R. 1990. Stratification, emotional energy and the transient emotions, in *Research Agendas in the Sociology of Emotions*, edited by T.D. Kemper. Albany: State University of New York Press, 27–57.
Collins, R. 2004. *Interaction Ritual Chains*. Princeton: Princeton University Press.
Collinson, D. 1992. *Managing the Shopfloor*. Berlin: Walter de Gruyter.
Coser, R.L. 1960. Laughter among Colleagues. A Study of the Social Functions of Humour among the Staff of a Mental Hospital. *Psychiatry*, 23, 81–95.
Craib, I. 1998. *Experiencing Identity*. London: Sage Publications.
Currie, J., Thiele, B. and Harris, P. 2002. *Gendered Universities in Globalized Economies*. Lanham: Lexington Books.
Damasio, A. 2000. *The Feeling of What Happens: Body and Emotion in the Making of Consciousness*. London: William Heinemann.
Daston, L. 1995. The Moral Economy of Science. *OSIRIS*, 10, 3–24.
Douglas, M. 1975. *Implicit Meanings*. London: Routledge & Kegan Paul.
Durkheim, E. [1905]1952. *Suicide*. London: Routledge.
Ehn, B. and Löfgren, O. 2004. *Hur blir man klok på universitetet?* Lund: Studenterlitteratur.
Elias, N. 1978. *What is Sociology?* London: Hutchinson.
Fanelli, D. 2010. Do Pressures to Publish Increase Scientists' Bias? *PLoS ONE*, 5(4), e10271.
Fineman, S. (ed.) 1993. *Emotions in Organizations*. London: Sage.
Fineman, S. (ed.) 2000. *Emotions in Organizations*. 2nd Edition. London: Sage.
Flam, H. 1990a. Emotional 'Man', in 'Man' and the Problem of Collective Action. *International Sociology*, 5(1), 39–56.
Flam, H. 1990b. Emotional 'Man': II. Corporate Actors as Emotion-Motivated Emotion Managers. *International Sociology*, 5 (2), 225–34.
Flam, H. 2002. Corporate emotions and emotions in corporations, in *Emotions and Sociology*, edited by J. Barbalet. Oxford: Blackwell Publishing, 90–113.
Fox, S. 1990. The Ethnography of Humour and the Problem of Social Reality. *Sociology*, 24(3), 431–46.
Francis, L.E. 1994. Laughter, the Best Meditation: Humor as Emotion Management in Interaction. *Symbolic Interaction*, 17(2), 147–63.
Freud, S. [1922]1999. *Wit and its Relation to the Unconscious*. Florence, KY: Routledge.
Gerholm, L. and Gerholm, T. 1992. *Doktorshatten*. Stockholm: Carlssons Bokförlag.

Gibson, D.E. 1997. The Struggle for Reason: The Sociology of Emotions in Organizations. *Social Perspectives on Emotion*, Vol. 4, 211–56.

Giorgi, A., Fischer, C.T. and Murray, E.L. (eds) 1975. *Duquesne Studies in Phenomenological Psychology*, Vol. 1. Pittsburg: Duquesne University Press.

Giorgi, A. 1992. Description versus Interpretation: Competing Alternative Strategies for Qualitative Research. *Journal of Phenomenological Psychology*, 23(2), 119–35.

Goffman, E. 1951. Symbols of Class Status. *British Journal of Sociology*, 2, 294–304.

Goffman, E. 1967. *Interaction Ritual*. London: Penguin Books.

Gottschalk, L., Winget, C.N. and Gleser, G. 1969. *Manual for Using the Gottschalk-Gleser Content Analysis Scales*. Berkeley: University of California Press.

Gulbrandsen, J.M. 2000. *Research Quality and Organisational Factors: An Investigation of the Relationship*. Trondheim: Department of Industrial Economics and Technology Management, NTNU.

Haavind, H. 1998. Understanding women in the psychological mode: the challenge from the experiences of Nordic women, in *Is There a Nordic Feminism?*, edited by D. Von der Fehr, B. Rosenbeck and A.G. Jónasdottir. Berkeley: University of California Press, 243–72.

Hagstrom, W.O. 1972. Gift-Giving as an Organizing Principle in Science, in *Sociology of Science*, edited by B. Barnes. London: Penguin Books, 105–21.

Harré, R. 1986. *The Social Construction of Emotions*. Oxford: Basil Blackwell.

Hasse, C. 2003. Kropstegns betydning i uddannelseskulturer, in *Akademisk Tilblivelse*, edited by L. Højgard and D.M. Søndergaard. København: Akademisk Forlag, 159–89.

Hatch, M.J. and Ehrlich, S.B. 1993. Spontanous Humour as an Indicator of Paradox and Ambiguity in Organizations. *Organization Studies*, 14(4), 505–26.

Henningsen, I. and Højgård, L. 2002. The Leaking Pipeline. *Dansk Sociologi*, 13 (2), 25–51.

Henriksson, M. et al. 2000. I vetenskapens namn: Et minnesarbete. *Kvinnovetenskaplig Tidskrift*, 1, 5–25.

Hochschild, A.R. 1983. *The Managed Heart*. Berkeley: University of California Press.

Hochschild, A.R. 2003. *The Commercialization of Intimate Life*. London: University of California Press.

Holm, L. 2001. The social context of eating, in *Eating Patterns: A Day in the Lives of Nordic Peoples*, edited by U. Kjärnes. Report No. 7, SIFO, 159–99.

Jacobsen, B. 2001a. *Hvad er god forskning?* København: Hans Reitzels Forlag.

Jacobsen, B., Madsen, M.B. and Vincent, C. 2001b. *Danske Forskningsmiljøer. En undersøgelse af universitetsforsknin-gens aktuelle situation*. København: Hans Reitzels Forlag.

James, W. [1884]1983. *Essays on Psychology*, edited by Frederick H. Burkhardt, Fredson Bowers and Ignas K. Skrupskelis. Cambridge, MA: Harvard University Press.

Jensen, H.N. 2000. *Working conditions and career ambitions and possibilities between Ph.D. students. Myths or realities about 'gendered' Ph.D. students*. Paper AARE Sydney Conference 4–7. December, The University of Sydney.
Jensen, H.N. 2003. Danske ph.d.-studerendes karrierespor – vejen ad hvilken, in *Akademisk Tilblivelse*, edited by L. Højgard and D.M. Søndergaard. København: Akademisk Forlag, 101–21.
Kemper, T.D. 1978a. *A Social Interactional Theory of Emotions*. New York: John Wiley.
Kemper, T.D. 1978b. Toward a Sociology of Emotions. *American Sociologist*, 13, 30–41.
Kemper, T.D. 1982. Social Constructionist and Positivist Approaches to the Sociology of Emotions. *American Journal of Sociology*, 87, 336–61.
Kemper, T.D. and Collins, R. 1990. Dimensions of Microinteraction. *American Journal of Sociology*, 96(1), 32–68.
Kemper, T.D. 2002. Predicting emotions in groups: Some lessons from September 11, in *Emotions and Sociology*, edited by J. Barbalet. Oxford: Blackwell Publishing.
Knorr, K.D., Mittermeir, R., Aichholzer, G. and Waller, G. 1979. Leadership and group performances: a positive relationship in academic units, in *Scientific Productivity*, edited by F.M. Andrews. Cambridge: Cambridge University Press, 95–120.
Knorr-Cetina, K. 1982. Scientific Communities or transepistemic arenas of research? *Social Studies of Science*, 12, 101–30.
Knorr-Cetina, K. 1999. *Epistemic Cultures: How the Sciences make Knowledge*. Cambridge: Harvard University Press.
Koestler, A. 1964. *The Act of Creation*. London: Hutchinson.
Krejsler, J. 2007. Discursive strategies that individualize: CVs and appraisal interviews. *International Journal of Qualitative Studies in Education*, 20(4), 473–90.
Krejsler, J. 2011. Moderniseringsmaskinen. Universitetsrefor-mer og nye spillerum for akademikeren, in *Motivation og mismod. Det nye arbejdslivs dilemmaer*, edited by K.M. Bovbjerg, Århus Universitetsforlag, 237–63
Lewis, H.B. 1971. *Shame and Guilt in Neurosis*. New York: International University Press.
Lutz, C.A. 1988. *Unnatural Emotions*. Chicago: Chicago University Press.
Maanen, J. Van and Kunda, G. 1989. Real feelings: emotional expression and organizational culture in *Research in Organizational Behaviour*, edited by B.M. Staw and L. Cummings. Greenwich, CT: JAI Press, 11, 43–103.
Martinson B.C., Anderson, M.A. and Vries, R. 2005. Scientists behaving badly. *Nature*, 435(9), 737–8.
Molin, M. and Åsel, M. 1996. *Att leva eller forska eller att leva och forska. En undersökning av yngre doktoranders arbettsmiljö ved Umeå Universitet*. Rapport från universitetshälsan, Umeå.
Mulkay, M. 1988. *On Humour*. Oxford: Polity Press.

Nathanson, D.L. 1992. *Shame and Pride*. New York: W.W. Norton & Company.
Nowotny, H. and Taschwer, K. (eds) 1996. *The Sociology of the Sciences*. Cheltenham (UK) and Brookfield (US): Edward Elgar Publishing Company, Vols. I and II.
Nyend, F. and Wennes, G. 2005. *Kan organisationer føle?* Oslo: Cappelen Akademisk Forlag.
Pierce, J.L. 1995. *Gender Trials*. Berkeley: University of California Press.
Pizzini, F. 1991. Communication hierarchies in humour: gender differences in the obstetrical/gynaecological setting. *Discourse & Society*, 2(4), 477–88.
Poder, P. 2004. *Feelings of Power and the Power of Feelings – Handling Emotion in Organisational Change*. Ph.d.-afhandling, København: Sociologisk Institut.
Radcliffe-Brown, A.R. 1952. *Structure and Function in Primitive Society*. New York: The Free Press.
Retzinger, S.M. 1991. *Violent Emotions*. London: Sage.
Rivera, J. de 1992. Emotional Climate: Social structure and emotional dynamics, in *International Review of Studies on Emotions*. New York: John Wiley & Sons, 197–218.
Scheff, T.J. 1990. *Microsociology*. Chicago, London: University of Chicago Press.
Scheff, T.J. 1994. *Bloody Revenge*. Oxford: Westview Press.
Scheff, T.J. 1995. Academic Gangs. *Crime, Law and Social Change*, 23, 157–62.
Scheff, T.J. 1997. *Emotions, the Social Bond, and Human Reality*. Cambridge: Cambridge University Press.
Schoug, F. 2002. Vetenskabssamhället som konkurrenssystem. *RIG Kulturhistorisk Tidskrift*, 2, 73–94.
Schoug, F. 2003. De effektiva lärjungarna: Politiska reformer och akademisk praktik, in *Den vildväxande högskolan*, edited by L. Kim and P. Mårtens. Stockholm: Nya Doxa, 205–37.
Schoug, F. 2004. *På trappans första steg*. Lund: Studenterlitteratur.
Shott, S. 1979. Emotion and Social Life: A Symbolic Interactionist Analysis. *American Journal of Sociology*, 84(6), 1317–34.
Simmel, G. [1908]1970. *Kamp*. Uppsala: Argos.
Simmel, G. [1910]1997: Sociology of the Meal, in *Simmel on Culture*, edited by D. Friesby and M. Featherstone. London: Sage, 130–5.
Simmel, G. [1917]1950. Sociability, in *The Sociology of Georg Simmel*, edited by K.H. Volff. London: The Free Press of Glencoe, 40–57.
Singh, P. and Krishnaiah, V.S.R. 1989. Analysis of Work Climate Perceptions and Performance of Research and Developmental Units. *Scientometrics*, 17(3–4), 333–51.
Snow, C.P. 1959. *The Two Cultures and the Scientific Revolution*. Cambridge: Cambridge University Press.
Stoppard, J.M. and Gruchy, C.D. 1993. Gender, Context, and Expression of Positive Emotions. *Personality and Social Psychology Bulletin*, 19(2), 143–50.
Søndergaard, D.M. 1994. Køn som metaprincip. *Kvinder, Køn og Forskning*, 3(3), 40–63.

Søndergaard, D.M. 1996. *Tegnet på kroppen*. København: Museum Tusculanums Forlag.
Tagiuri, R. 1968. The Concept of Organizational Climate, in *Organizational Climate*, edited by R. Tagiuri and G.H. Litwin. Boston: Harvard University.
Thoits, P.A. 1990. Emotional Deviance: Research Agendas, in *Research Agendas in the Sociology of Emotions*, edited by T. Kemper. Albany: State University of New York Press, 180–203.
Thoits, P.A. 1996. Managing the emotions of others. *Symbolic Interaction*, 19(2), 85–109.
Thoits, P.A. 2004. Emotion Norms, Emotion Work and Social Order, in *Feelings and Emotions*, edited by A.S.R. Manstead, N. Frijda and A. Fischer. Cambridge: Cambridge University Press, 359–81.
Tomkins, S.S. 1962. *Affect/Imagery/Consciousness*, Vol. I. New York: Springer.
Toren, N. 2000. *Hurdles in the Halls of Science*. Lanham: Lexington Books.
Wagner, W. 1977. *Angst og bluff på universitetet*. København: Tiderne Skifter.
Waldron, V.R. 2000. Relational Experiences and Emotion at Work, in *Emotion in Organizations*, edited by S. Fineman. London: Sage, 64–82.
Wouters, C. 1992. On Status Competition and Emotional Management: the Study of Emotions as a New Field. *Theory, Culture and Society*, 9 (1), 229–59.
Weber, M. [1930]1995. *The Protestant Ethic and the Spirit of Capitalism*. London: Routledge.
Williams, S.J. 1998. 'Capitalising' on emotions? Rethinking the Inequalities in Health Debate. *Sociology*, 23(1), 121–41.
Wright, S. 2009. What counts? The skewing effects of research assessment systems. *Nordic Studies in Education*, Special, 18–33.
Zijderveld, A.C. 1968. Jokes and their relation to social reality. *Social Research*, 35, 286–311.

Index

Academia
    hierarchical power structure of 8–9
    specific structure of 8
academic rapier (metaphor) 56–7
academic space 29–30
academics, emotional ambivalence of 136
anger
    appointment committees as cause of 60–4
    assessors' 58–60
    explosive, and warfare 103–5
    and gender 125–8
    helpless, and withdrawal 102–3
    peer reviews 99–101
    unacknowledged shame 98
Appel, M. 24, 30, 34
appointment committees
    anger caused by 60–4
    system of 62n5
Asplund, Johan 105
assessment, academic
    anger and shame 99–101
    argument for the sake of argument 56–7
    assessed, anger of 60–4
    assessors, anger of 58–60
    distrust 65–6
    enjoyment of 60
    envy 66–8
    helpless/explosive anger 101–4
    importance of 56
    objectivity of 59–60
    personal and emotional criteria, role of 60
    purpose of 56
    schadenfreude 68
assistant professors
    appointment and promotion 38n2
    deceiving game 41–6
    facade, academic 43–4
    fear and doubt of 41–3
    friendliness as feeling rule 37–41
    joking relationships between 76–9, 129–31
    mistakes, punishment of 43
    pride, cultural regulation of 45–52
    solidarity and competition 51–2
    ventriloquism 45–52
associate professors
    deceiving game, alternatives to 119–20
    joking relationships between 76–9, 129–31
    and professors, comparison 56n2
    wearing/nourishing relationships 109–11

Barbalet, Jack 11n11, 137
Becher, T. 14, 65n6
Ben-Ze'ev, A. 66
bimodal alienation 99, 106
biological approach to emotions 7, 7n1, 11n10
Bloch, C. 97n1, 99n3, 113n1, 115n4,
Bourdieu, Pierre 8–9, 50, 94, 116
Bowen, M. 98
Buber, M. 98
bypassed shame 98

clan structures among professors 106n6
Clark, Candace 10, 113–16
cognitive techniques 27–8
Cole, S. 56n1
collective space 30–2
Collins, Randahl 9, 9n6, 87, 89, 90
community, PhD 30–2
competence, laughter and humour as 71–3
competition
    distrust as result of 65–6
    envy as result of 66–8
    feelings arising from 55

humour as mirror image of 79
   intensification of 139–40
   and prohibition against pride 51–2
   schadenfreude as result of 68
   and solidarity between PhD fellows 32–3
conceptual framework 11–12, 12
conversational norms 88–9
counter-groups, academic 31–2
cultural approach to emotions 10–11, 11n10
cultures, research, urban/rural 14–15, 65–6, 65n6

Daston, Lorraine 10n8
data collection 13
deceiving game 41–6, 107, 116–20
departmental atmosphere 136–7
discursive-constructivist approach to emotions 7, 7n2
discussion groups, academic 31–2
distrust as result of competition 65–6
doubt
   assistant professors 41–3
   experienced by PhD fellows 18–19
   and gender 116–20
Douglas, Mary 82, 83

eating together 85–6
Ehn, B. 56, 60, 112
Elias, Norbert 98
emotion work
   academic space 29–30
   collective space 30–2
   defined 26–7
   following peer reviews 63–4
   private space 27–8
   segmented 27–32
   success of 34
emotional ambivalence of academics 136
emotional intelligence 140–1
emotional micropolitics
   anger and gender 125–8
   fear/doubt and gender 116–20
   feeling rules as gendered 115–16
   gender and social place 132–3
   laughter and humour 128–32
   Me First strategy 114–15, 117, 121, 125
   micropolitics concept 114, 115
   pride and gender 121–4
   social place concept 113–16
   You First strategy 115
emotions
   approaches to research on 7–12, 12
   and scientific research 138
   self-asserting/self-transcending 137–8, 139–40
engulfment 98–9, 106–7
envy as result of competition 66–8
expression rules 10
externalism 34

facade, academic 43–4
feeling processes 11–12, 12
feeling rules 10
   friendliness 37–41
   as gendered 115–16
femininity *see* gender
Flam, H. 10
Freud, Sigmund 82
friendliness, politics of 37–41, 107

gang structures among professors 106n6
gender
   and anger 125–8
   as constructed distinction 115–16
   deceiving game 116–20
   and fear and doubt 116–20
   feeling rules 115–16
   joking relationships 77, 129–32
   and pride, cultural regulation of 121–4
   and social place 132–3
gift-giving, research as form of 51
gloating over setbacks 68
Goffman, E. 86
ground floor humour of PhD fellows 73–6, 128–9

Haavind, H. 115, 116
Hagstrom, W.O. 51
helplessness, anger of 102–3
Henriksson, M. 26n11
hierarchical power structure of Academia 8–9, 91–4
Hochschild, Arlie 10, 10n9, 11n10, 27n12, 44n5

humour
  as arising from contrasts and contradictions 82–3
  as challenging hierarchy 75–6
  as competence 71–3, 83
  emotional micropolitics 128–32
  ground floor humour of PhD fellows 73–6, 128–9
  as integrative/subversive 83
  joking relationships 76–9
  as leadership tool 79–82
  as mirror image of competition 79
  poking fun at academic ideals 78
  and solidarity 108
  see also lunchroom interaction

interactional approach to emotions 7, 7n3
internalism 34
interviews 13, 13n15, 18n3
isolation
  and damaged relationships 109–11
  of PhD fellows 19
  as social bond 98, 101–6

Jacobson, Bo 136–7
jealousy as result of competition 66–8
Jensen, Hanne Nexø 20, 34n15
joking relationships 76–9, 95–6, 129–31

Kemper, Theodor 9, 9n6, 20
Koestler, A. 82

laughter and humour
  as arising from contrasts and contradictions 82–3
  as challenging hierarchy 75–6
  as competence 71–3, 83
  emotional micropolitics 128–32
  ground floor humour of PhD fellows 73–6, 128–9
  as integrative/subversive 83
  joking relationships 76–9
  as leadership tool 79–82
  as mirror image of competition 79
  poking fun at academic ideals 78
  and solidarity 108
  see also lunchroom interaction
leadership, humour as tool in 79–82

Lewis, H.B. 98
lunchroom interaction
  conversational norms 88–9
  fellowship in 87–90
  fusion of hierarchy and fellowship 94
  hierarchy in 91–4
  as interaction ritual 87
  lunch as social form 85–7
  solidarity 90

masculinity *see* gender
Me First strategy 114–15, 117–18, 125
meals 85–6
methodology for research 12–13
micropolitics, concept of 114
mistakes, punishment of 43
modernisation of universities 139–40

Nathanson, D.L. 82
nepotism 63
neutrality 29–30
new public management 139
not-greeting 105
nourishing/wearing relationships 108–11

'old boys' networks 63
open non-differentiated shame 98

peer reviews
  academic rapier (metaphor) 56–7
  anger and shame 99–101
  argument for the sake of argument 56–7
  assessed, anger of 60–4
  assessors, anger of 58–60
  distrust 65–6
  enjoyment of 60
  envy 66–8
  helpless/explosive anger 101–4
  importance of 55
  objectivity of 56, 56n1, 59–60
  personal and emotional criteria, role of 60
  purpose of 55
  schadenfreude 68
  see also supervisor relationships
PhD fellows
  academic space 29–30

collective space 30–2, 73–6
deceiving game, alternatives to 118–19
ground floor humour of 73–6, 128–9
internalists/externalists 34
isolation of 19
power, displays of experienced by 20, 21–4
power structure, emotions of 24–6
private space 27–8
programmes 17n1
projects as weapons between colleagues 24–6
research, emotions of 17–20
segmentation of emotions 26–32
solidarity and competition between 32–3
uncertainty and doubt of 18–19
see also lunchroom interaction
Pizzini, F. 80, 92
plagiarism 65–6, 65n6
politics of friendliness 37–41, 107
positive thinking 27–8
Poder, Poul 27
power
displays of experienced by PhD fellows 20, 21–4
structure, emotions of 24–6
pride, cultural regulation of 45–52, 94–5, 107–8, 121–4
private space 27–8
professors
and associate professors, comparison 56n2
deceiving game, alternatives to 119–20

Radcliffe-Brown, A.R. 83
recognition, academic 45–52, 94–5, 107–8, 121–4
relational emotions 13, 13n14
representative emotions 10
research
emotions of 17–20
impact of emotions on 138
research cultures, urban/rural 14–15, 65–6, 65n6
Retzinger, S.M. 99n2
rural/urban research environments 14–15, 65–6, 65n6

schadenfreude as result of competition 68
Scheff, Thomas 10, 11n12, 99n2, 106, 106n6
Schoug, Fredrik 34
scientific research and emotions 138
scientific theft 65–6, 65n6
segmentation of emotions
academic space 29–30
collective space 30–2
defined 26–7
private space 27–8
success of 34
selection of interviewees 13, 13n15
self-asserting emotions 137, 139–40
self-transcending emotions 137–8, 139–40
shame 97–8, 99–101, 99n2
Shields, S.A. 127
shop floor humour 73
Simmel, Georg 55, 85–6, 88, 90
social bonds in academia
engulfment 98–9, 106–7
isolation 98, 101–6
nourishing/wearing relationships 108–11
shame 97–8
solidarity 98–9, 107–8
theory 97–9
three forms of 98–9
social place 113–16, 132–3
social responsiveness, theory of 105
solidarity
and assessors' anger 59
and competition between PhD fellows 32–3
lunchroom interaction 90
and prohibition against pride 51–2
as social bond 98, 107–8
Søndergaard, D.M. 115, 116
specific structure of Academia 8
spirals of emotion 98, 99–101
status denigration by supervisors 21–4, 31
strategy, friendliness as 37–41
structural approach to emotions 8–10
stupid, fear of being labelled as 43
supervisor relationships
concealment of problems with 30
importance of 24
nature of 20

power, displays of experienced by PhD
    fellows 20, 21–4
  satisfactory 20–1
  see also peer reviews

teaching, pride in success with 46–7
theoretical framework 7–12, 12
Tomkins, S.S. 82
Trowler, P.R. 14, 65n6

unacknowledged shame 98
uncertainty
  assistant professors 41–3
  and gender 116–20

PhD fellows 18–19
universities, modernisation of 139–40
urban/rural research environments 14–15,
    65–6, 65n6

ventriloquism 45–52, 94–5, 107–8,
    121–4

Waldron, V.R. 112
wearing/nourishing relationships 108–11
withdrawal 102–3
Wouters, Cas 86

You First strategy 115

Printed in Dunstable, United Kingdom